D0146426

Who Is God?

Acadia Studies in Bible and Theology

H. Daniel Zacharias, General Editor

The last several decades have witnessed dramatic developments in biblical and theological study. Full-time academics can scarcely keep up with fresh discoveries, ongoing archaeological work, new exegetical proposals, experiments in methods and hermeneutics, the rise of majority world theology, and innovative theological proposals and syntheses. For students and nonspecialists, these developments can be confusing and daunting. What has been needed is a series of succinct studies that assess these issues and present their findings in a way that students, pastors, laity, and nonspecialists will find accessible and rewarding. Acadia Studies in Bible and Theology, sponsored by Acadia Divinity College in Wolfville, Nova Scotia, and in conjunction with the college's Hayward Lectureship, constitutes such a series.

The Hayward Lectureship has brought to Acadia many distinguished scholars of Bible and theology, such as Sir Robin Barbour, James D. G. Dunn, C. Stephen Evans, Edith Humphrey, Leander Keck, Helmut Koester, Richard Longenecker, Martin Marty, Jaroslav Pelikan, John Webster, Randy Woodley, and N. T. Wright. Initiated by Lee M. McDonald and Craig A. Evans, the Acadia Studies in Bible and Theology series continues to reflect this rich heritage and foundation.

These studies are designed to guide readers through the ever more complicated maze of critical, interpretative, and theological discussion taking place today. But these studies are not introductory in nature; nor are they mere surveys. Authored by leading authorities in the field, the Acadia Studies in Bible and Theology series offers critical assessments of major issues that the church faces in the twenty-first century. Readers will gain the requisite orientation and fresh understanding of the important issues that will enable them to take part meaningfully in discussion and debate.

Who Is God?

Key Moments *of* Biblical Revelation

Richard Bauckham

B
Baker Academic
a division of Baker Publishing Group
Grand Rapids, Michigan

Published by Baker Academic
a division of Baker Publishing Group
PO Box 6287, Grand Rapids, MI 49516-6287
www.bakeracademic.com

Printed in the United States of America

Library of Congress Cataloging-in-Publication Data
Names: Bauckham, Richard, author.
Title: Who is God? : key moments of biblical revelation / Richard Bauckham.
Description: Grand Rapids, Michigan : Baker Academic, a division of Baker Publishing Group, 2020. | Series: Acadia studies in Bible and theology | Includes bibliographical references and index.
Identifiers: LCCN 2019048615 | ISBN 9781540961907 (cloth)
Subjects: LCSH: God—Biblical teaching.
Classification: LCC BS544 .B385 2020 | DDC 231—dc23

ISBN 978-1-5409-6193-8 (ITPE)

21 22 23 24 25 26 7 6 5 4 3

In keeping with biblical principles of creation stewardship, Baker Publishing Group advocates the responsible use of our natural resources. As a member of the Green Press Initiative, our company uses recycled paper when possible. The text paper of this book is composed in part of post-consumer waste.

Contents

Preface

The origins of this book lie in three lectures that I gave twice, first as the Frumentius Lectures for 2015 at the Ethiopian Graduate School of Theology in Addis Ababa and second as the Hayward Lectures for 2018 at Acadia Divinity College in Nova Scotia, Canada. The lectures formed the basis for chapters 2, 3, and 4 of this book, for which purpose they were revised and somewhat expanded. Chapter 1 has been written *de novo* for this book.

I am grateful to those who invited me to give the two lecture series, as well as to those who in both places made me very welcome, formed enthusiastic audiences, and asked thoughtful and probing questions.

Because the book originated as lectures, I have not provided footnotes with references to the secondary literature. The footnotes are limited to biblical references and brief explanatory notes. But at the end of each chapter I have provided bibliographic notes, indicating some of the more important and helpful published work on the subjects of that chapter. Of course, because the chapters range widely over biblical passages and themes, I could have extended the bibliography indefinitely. I decided not to list commentaries because there are so many good commentaries and readers can more easily find them for themselves.

Introduction

In our ever more secular age many people pose the question "Does God exist?" or "Is there a God?" But to consider this question seriously we must also ask the question "Who is God?" The content that people give to the word "god" has varied and still varies enormously, and so one has to ask, "What kind of God are you actually talking about?" "What God?" or "Who is God?" In biblical times this was the obvious question. Very few people thought there was nothing to which one could apply the term "god" or "the gods" or "the divine." But which god was truly God? Who is the God you are talking about? This was the key question and I think still is.

Even though all notions of the divine have something in common, and some more than others, Christians give priority to those key events and experiences that the Bible relates and expounds as the revelation of God. We can answer the question "Who is God?" only by attending to who God has revealed himself to be. To this the whole biblical revelation is relevant. Asked what the whole Bible is about, I would say it is most centrally about the identity of God, while at the same time it tells the story of God and his creation, that all-encompassing story that extends from creation in the beginning to new creation at the end. Intensively the Bible is about the identity of God; extensively it tells the story of God and the world.

Within that all-encompassing story, there are key moments of revelation that could be said to define who God is for us—or, it would be better to say, moments in which God defines who God is for us. These are not merely moments that are narrated once within the biblical story; they are more like reference points to which the rest of Scripture constantly refers back. They are moments that reverberate through the whole story. Moreover, like all events of great significance, their significance is not grasped all at once and forever. They are moments whose meaning is never exhausted. So we should read them as events pregnant with meaning, pointing us finite creatures of God to God's inexhaustible and mysterious identity. They should challenge our own understanding of God and our own relationship with God, for, as J. B. Phillips famously said, "Your God is too small."[1]

The key moments of divine disclosure we shall reflect on in this book are by no means the only such moments in the Bible. Others could have been chosen. But those we consider here are undoubtedly among the most significant. They are Jacob's dream at Bethel (Gen. 28:10–22), the revelation to Moses at the burning bush (Exod. 3), the revelation to Moses on Mount Sinai (Exod. 33:17–34:8), and the three key moments of revelation in the Gospel of Mark (1:9–11; 9:2–8; 15:37–39). In all these cases our exploration of biblical theology will range more widely than these moments of disclosure themselves, but they will be our guiding stars by which to travel through related territory.

My approach in this book is to treat the Bible as a canonical whole. Here I do not engage in historical reconstruction

1. J. B. Phillips, *Your God Is Too Small: A Guide for Believers and Skeptics Alike* (New York: Touchstone, 2004). This book was first published in 1952.

behind and around the texts, though that is a task that greatly interests me and that I pursue elsewhere. Here I am interested in the texts as we have them and as belonging to the canon of Scripture—a collection of sacred writings that witness to God through the divine disclosures they contain.

I hope to show readers that the Bible's account of the identity of God is consistent both within and across the two testaments. I have no wish to discount the diversity of the various parts of Scripture, but I think that a theological interpretation of Scripture should seek the unity in the diversity. The approach is necessarily broad brush, but detailed exegesis is at its heart. The exegesis aims to do justice to particular passages in their own literary contexts, while at the same time highlighting those themes that play an important role in the canon as a whole.

This is a small book on a vast and vastly important topic. Nevertheless, I dare to hope that, by God's grace, it may help some readers to know God better.

1

The Revelation of the Divine Presence

The first key moment of revelation that we shall consider is the dream of the patriarch Jacob, ancestor of the people of Israel, at Bethel:

> [10]Jacob left Beer-sheba and went toward Haran. [11]He came to a
> certain place and stayed there for the night, because the sun had
> set. Taking one of the stones of the place, he put it under his
> head and lay down in that place. [12]And he dreamed that there
> was a ladder set up on the earth, the top of it reaching to heaven;
> and the angels of God were ascending and descending on it.
> [13]And the LORD stood beside him and said, "I am the LORD, the
> God of Abraham your father and the God of Isaac; the land on
> which you lie I will give to you and to your offspring; [14]and your
> offspring shall be like the dust of the earth, and you shall spread
> abroad to the west and to the east and to the north and to the
> south; and all the families of the earth shall be blessed in you
> and in your offspring. [15]Know that I am with you and will keep
> you wherever you go, and will bring you back to this land; for I

> will not leave you until I have done what I have promised you." [16]Then Jacob woke from his sleep and said, "Surely the LORD is in this place—and I did not know it!" [17]And he was afraid, and said, "How awesome is this place! This is none other than the house of God, and this is the gate of heaven."
>
> [18]So Jacob rose early in the morning, and he took the stone that he had put under his head and set it up for a pillar and poured oil on the top of it. [19]He called that place Bethel; but the name of the city was Luz at the first. [20]Then Jacob made a vow, saying, "If God will be with me, and will keep me in this way that I go, and will give me bread to eat and clothing to wear, [21]so that I come again to my father's house in peace, then the LORD shall be my God, [22]and this stone, which I have set up for a pillar, shall be God's house; and of all that you give me I will surely give one-tenth to you." (Gen. 28:10–22)[1]

The story is well known, but it is not usually seen to have the pivotal role in the whole biblical story that I shall suggest in this chapter. Of course, God had appeared and spoken many times to Jacob's grandfather Abraham and on occasion to his father, Isaac, also. God had promised to give the land to their descendants, that they would have innumerable descendants, and that through their descendants blessing would come to all the nations. But only to Isaac did God reveal that God was "with" him (Gen. 26:24, cf. 26:28).[2] This promise of personal presence then comes to much fuller expression in Jacob's dream at Bethel. On this occasion God repeats the promises made to Abraham and Isaac, personalizing them as promises to Jacob and *his* descendants (28:13–14), but the focus of both what

1. All Scripture quotations are from the NRSV, unless otherwise indicated.

2. According to Gen. 21:20, "God was with" Ishmael, while according to Gen. 21:22, "God is with" Abraham, but in neither case is this a revelation of God's presence made to that person.

Jacob sees and what he hears God say is the revelation of God's presence with him. It is a revelation that, as we shall see, anticipates much that the rest of the Bible has to say about the presence of God with humans.

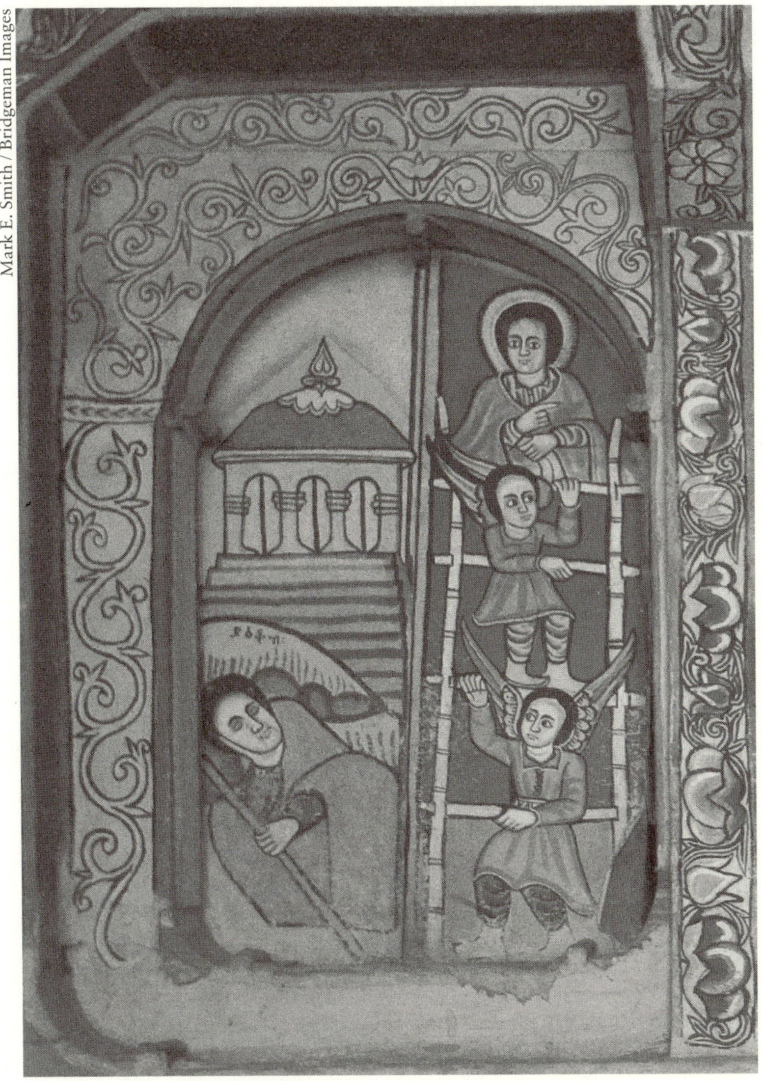

Mark E. Smith / Bridgeman Images

Figure 1. Jacob's Ladder. Debre Sina Maryam Church, Gorgora, Ethiopia

When Jacob arrived at Bethel, he was in flight from his family home and the anger of his brother, Esau. Jacob had tricked Isaac into giving his blessing to Jacob rather than to Esau, and his mother, Rebekah, had sent him away, for his own safety, on a very long journey to the home of her relatives, some five hundred miles away as the crow flies. It was a daunting journey to an unknown future, and Jacob was for the first time in his life truly on his own. It was a situation that required a change in his relationship with God, whom he had known hitherto as the family God, the God of Abraham and Isaac (Gen. 28:13). If Jacob is now to find himself apart from his family, if he is to find who he can be in this newly uncertain world in which he is alone, he must also now find God as his own God. Not that he thinks of this for himself. It is not Jacob who turns to God but God who turns to Jacob.

The image Jacob sees in his dream is probably not, as most of the translations have it, a ladder but a staircase (which the Hebrew word can equally well mean). Probably it is a broad stone staircase running up the stepped side of one of the artificial mountains—known as ziggurats—that the people of ancient Mesopotamia built. There was a famous ziggurat in the city of Ur, from which Jacob's ancestors came. The gods were thought to live at the top of the cosmic mountain that touches heaven. So, in order to worship them, the Sumerians would build a great mound on which to place a temple, so that the gods could dwell there and the people could worship the gods by ascending the steps to the summit of the mountain.

What is remarkable about Jacob's dream is that he sees God not, as one would expect, at the top of the stairway but at the bottom. This is the most likely meaning of the words that could be translated "the LORD stood above it" (i.e., the staircase) but most probably mean "the LORD stood beside him" (i.e., Jacob;

Gen. 28:13). This is the translation that coheres with what the Lord says to Jacob: "I am with you" (28:15). Jacob does not have to make the arduous ascent up the staircase to meet with God at the top. Nor does God's communication with Jacob have to be mediated by the angels who are passing up and down the staircase. They are the divine messengers ("angel" means "messenger") who are sent from heaven to do God's will on earth. They symbolize communication between heaven and earth. But in Jacob's dream God has, as it were, bypassed them. He himself has come down the staircase and stands looking at Jacob sleeping beside him. He is not remote in heaven but down on earth "with" Jacob.

So when Jacob wakes in wonder, the dream still filling his consciousness, he says, "This is none other than the house of God" (Gen. 28:17). He means that where God is to be found is not only in heaven but on the very spot where he has been sleeping: "Surely the LORD is in this place—and I did not know it!" (28:16). So the stone on which his head had rested while he dreamed he stands upright as a pillar and consecrates it as a memorial of God's presence there. He names the place Bethel, which means "the house of God." But even this recognition of God's presence there at Bethel does not reach the deepest meaning of Jacob's dream. What he has discovered is not so much that God is in that particular place as that God is where Jacob is. God is with Jacob and will be with him wherever he goes: "Know that I am with you and will keep you wherever you go" (28:15). God's revelation to Jacob is not for a man who is going to settle down at Bethel with a temple close at hand in which to worship God. Rather it is for a man on a journey. From now on every place where Jacob sleeps will be a Bethel. The leitmotif of Jacob's life will be God's presence with him (see Gen. 31:3; 35:3; 46:4).

We can see this in the rest of Jacob's story as Genesis tells it. When Jacob eventually returned to the land of promise, after fourteen years in the household of his uncle Laban, he reflected that God, as he had promised him at Bethel, truly "has been with me wherever I have gone" (Gen. 35:3). Jacob must have thought that that was the end of his travels outside the land of Canaan, but much later in his life he found he must make another long journey, this time to join his sons and their families in Egypt. For an old man such a journey would be more daunting than for a young man. Perhaps more importantly, it would be difficult for Jacob to understand how it could be part of God's purposes for him and his descendants. God had promised them this land. How could it be right for the whole family to settle in another country? And so once more God spoke to him "in visions of the night," assuring him that settling in Egypt really was a step on the way to God's promised future (46:3), and adding: "I myself will go down with you to Egypt" (46:4).

Finally, at the end of his very long life, Jacob looked back on God's unfailing and protective presence through all those years, speaking of "the God who has been my shepherd all my life to this day" (Gen. 48:15). The image harks back to Jacob's earlier life, when he had worked as a shepherd, looking after the flocks of his father-in-law, Laban (30:29–43). Jacob knew well what it meant to be a shepherd. The shepherd must lead his flock to pasture and water, but most fundamentally he must be with the flock at all times. He must be there with them in order to protect and care for them. Jacob's comparison of God with a shepherd inevitably reminds us of Psalm 23. At the heart of this psalm and of its image of God the shepherd are the words "for you are with me" (Ps. 23:4). In fact, they are literally the central words of this exquisitely composed poem. In a life with God, his guidance, provision, and protection are important, as Jacob and the psalmist knew, but in all such experiences the center and source is God's presence "with" us. The psalm helps make Jacob's experience available to all who pray it, and this must be the reason it has proved the most popular of all the psalms. To discover that God is "with" us is probably the most important discovery anyone can make, for, once made, it colors all of life's experiences.

So in the Bible, the little word "with," when it links God and humans, is a powerful word. In the Hebrew Bible, individual persons God promises to be "with" include Isaac, Joseph, Moses, Joshua, Gideon, Saul, David, Solomon, Jeroboam, Asa, Jehoshaphat, and Jeremiah.[3] God is also frequently said to be "with" the people of Israel when they are faithful to him.[4] Moreover, it appears that "The LORD be with you!" was a standard greeting in use in Israel.[5] It was how life should be, what one wished for oneself and for others. (This biblical usage has often been imitated in later history, not only in Christian liturgy but also in colloquial usage. Most English speakers who use the word "goodbye" as a signal of parting from someone are not aware that in its origins it meant "God be with you." A recent variation on it is the well-known phrase from Star Wars, "May the Force be with you!")

As the examples I have just listed will show, in the Old Testament God's presence "with" people is never a neutral or inactive presence that makes no difference. Sometimes it refers to

3. Isaac: Gen. 26:3, 24; Joseph: Gen. 48:21; cf. Acts 7:9; Moses: Exod. 3:12; Joshua: Deut. 31:23; Josh. 1:5, 9, 17; 3:7; Gideon: Judg. 6:12; Saul: 1 Sam. 10:7; 20:13; David: 2 Sam. 7:3, 9; Solomon: 1 Chron. 28:20; Jeroboam: 1 Kings 11:38; Asa: 2 Chron. 15:2; Jehoshaphat: 2 Chron. 20:17; Jeremiah: Jer. 1:8, 19. In the New Testament the expression is used of Jesus: John 3:2; 16:32; Acts 10:38. Only occasionally is the relationship stated the other way around (humans with God): Pss. 73:23; 139:18.

4. E.g., Deut. 2:7; 31:6, 8; 1 Kings 8:57; Pss. 46:7, 11; 91:15; Isa. 41:10; 43:2, 5; 45:14; Jer. 30:11; 42:11; 46:28; Amos 5:14; Hag. 1:13; 2:4; Zech. 8:23; 10:5.

5. Ruth 2:4; cf. Exod. 18:19; Judg. 6:12; 1 Sam. 17:37; 2 Sam. 14:17; 2 Chron. 36:23; Ezra 1:3; also Rom. 15:33; Phil. 4:9; 2 Thess. 3:16b; 2 Tim. 4:22.

protection and success in war. Always it refers to God's favor and care for those he chooses to be "with." It makes all the difference to their lives.

Understanding the Presence of God

In the Christian theological tradition, God's "omnipresence" has regularly featured as one of the metaphysical attributes of God, and it is not uncommon for Christians to say or to think "God is everywhere." This is not untrue, but we must be careful how we think about it. Because God is the Creator and Sustainer of the whole creation, God is immediately present to all his creatures, upholding their existence, and intimately involved in every event, enabling it to occur. This is God's universal presence as Creator. It does not mean that God is spatially extended throughout the world, as some people doubtless picture it. Nor is it merely a static "being there." God's presence is personal and active. He wills and acts to be present to every creature and at every moment. But this fundamental sense in which God is present to all creatures at all times in the same way is not the focus of concern in the Bible because, while it underlies our relationship with God, like everything else, we become conscious of it only when God engages with us as specific persons, whether individuals or groups. Even Psalm 139:7–10, which is often cited as biblical testimony to God's "omnipresence," is not concerned to affirm simply that "God is everywhere." What matters to the psalmist is that wherever he may go—even to the furthest reaches of the cosmos—God will find him there:

> Even there your hand shall lead me,
> and your right hand shall hold me fast. (v. 10)

It is a matter of God's fully personal and active presence *to* the psalmist in particular. The divine presence of which we can be aware is always particular.

The particularity of God's presence means that God may be present in many different ways. He may be present "with" individuals in their ongoing life, as he was with Jacob. He may be present in the pillar of cloud and fire that accompanied the Israelites after the exodus, guiding and protecting them. He may be present in the tabernacle in the wilderness and the temple in Jerusalem, where sacrifices enabled his people to enter his holy presence. God may appear in special theophanies, dreams, and visions, or even in the "sheer silence" in which he met with Elijah (1 Kings 19:12). All these are modes of God's gracious and succoring presence, but God may also be present in wrath and judgment against evil. Many of the varied forms of God's presence that we find in the Old Testament continue or have equivalents in the New Testament, but many of them also find their culmination in a new form of divine presence that surpasses them: incarnation, God's presence as the human Jesus Christ. Thereafter, the enduring form of God's presence with his people is as the Holy Spirit, the Spirit of Jesus Christ, present and active within believers.

Divine Presence—Accompanying and Static

The Bethel revelation has two aspects. So far I have stressed that for Jacob the experience of God's presence with him in one place provided the prospect of God's presence with him wherever he went. This is a pattern that others too may experience. A special experience of God's presence may inaugurate a life of living in the presence of God. After the initial experience, God may not usually be with the believer in the same evident way, but the believer may now be confident of God's accompanying presence in all the events of their life and open to the felt sense of that presence at least from time to time.

However, we should not neglect the fact that Jacob does call the place "the house of God." This term, which is otherwise used for a temple, suggests that God resides in that place. So, Jacob evidently thinks his dream revealed a continuous presence of God at Bethel, as well as the divine presence with Jacob wherever he goes. The stone Jacob set up marks that place as a shrine where God may be found. In fact, on Jacob's return to the land of Canaan, he also returns to Bethel and settles there for a time (Gen. 35:1, 6–7, 16). This time God actually instructs Jacob to build an altar at Bethel in order to worship (35:1, 14). This is the first time in the biblical narrative that God explicitly tells anyone to erect an altar (though such a command is implicit in 22:2). Later, Bethel was one of the shrines where Israelites worshiped in the period before the Jerusalem temple was established (Judg. 20:18, 26–27; 21:2) and then one of the two main shrines of the northern kingdom of Israel (1 Kings 12:26–33; 2 Kings 23:15–17; Hosea 10:15; Amos 3:14; 4:4; 7:13).

In using the phrase "the house of God," Jacob was adopting a common feature of ancient Near Eastern religion, which may also have been suggested in his dream: It was thought that a god could have an earthly house that corresponded to their house in heaven. The connection between the earthly house and the heavenly house ensured the presence of the god on earth. The temple was thus a place where people could be sure that they would come into the divine presence. The temple that Solomon built in Jerusalem conforms to this pattern.

But before there was an Israelite temple in Jerusalem, a permanent residence for God in a particular place, there was the tabernacle in the wilderness, created as part of God's covenant at Mount Sinai, when Israel became his special people. There is a significant parallel between the revelation of God to Jacob at Bethel and the two places where God resided "with" his people Israel: tabernacle and temple. The tabernacle corresponds to the ongoing, accompanying presence of God with Jacob wherever he went. The temple corresponds to the more permanent residence of God in his "house" at Bethel.

The English word "tabernacle" (from the Latin *tabernaculum*, "tent") is used in most English versions of the Hebrew Bible to translate a Hebrew word that means "dwelling" (*miškān*). It was given to Israel by God as a place where God would "dwell among them" (Exod. 29:46). Accordingly, in the wilderness it was situated in the middle of the Israelite encampment. But the tabernacle is also called a "sanctuary" or "holy place" (*miqdāš*; e.g., 25:8). This marks a major change from the period of the patriarchs in Genesis. In the accounts of the many encounters of the patriarchs and matriarchs with God, the words "holy" and "holiness" are never used. But once God, at Mount Sinai, has established a nation dedicated to him, holiness becomes a key feature of his presence among them. It means that impurity and sin cannot be tolerated in the divine presence. A system of "graded holiness"—whereby God's presence in the most holy place is separated from the profane space outside the tabernacle by less holy spaces—now serves to protect the people from the danger of the divine presence and, at the same time, to make God accessible to them. Through priestly mediation and sacrifices, God can be approached and his favor requested.

These features would apply also to the Jerusalem temple, but the distinguishing feature of the tabernacle, by comparison with the temple, is its mobility (see 2 Sam. 7:5–7). While God's people lived in tents and moved from place to place, so did God. Like God accompanying Jacob on his travels, so the tabernacle accompanied Israel. In fact, the movement of the cloud that manifested God's presence in the tabernacle not only accompanied but also guided the journey of the people through the wilderness (Num. 9:15–23).

Owing to its nomadic character, the tabernacle was not a "house" of God, still less a palace (though its rich adornment made it a tent fit for a king). The temple in Jerusalem, however, conceived by King David and built by his son Solomon, was both. The common word for "temple" (*hêkāl*) means a king's palace. In Jerusalem God's royal palace and the king's palace, God's rule over Israel and the king's rule on his behalf, were closely associated. Now that Israel was settled in the land, God's central presence with them no longer moved but found a "resting place" (Ps. 132:8) on Mount Zion, the place he chose for his dwelling (Deut. 12:5; Ps. 132:13). The Hebrew Bible as a whole leaves no doubt that this was God's intention.[6]

Some scholars writing biblical theology are inclined to denigrate the temple, comparing the idea of a static dwelling place for God unfavorably with the mobile tent. It ties God down, domesticates him, and puts him into the hands of the priests and their rituals, seen as means of controlling his presence and his grace. This view is probably influenced by a Protestant suspicion of holy places and sacerdotal rituals. But it is not true to the way the Bible itself views the temple. The plan of the temple and its system of priesthood and rituals are not fundamentally different from those of the tabernacle, though everything is on a grander scale. God "settles" on Mount Zion, not because the king and the priests wanted his presence under their control but because his people were now settled in the land. (When Solomon's temple was destroyed and God's people were exiled

6. In the New Testament, see Matt. 23:21; John 2:16–17; Acts 7:7.

from the land, God's presence once more traveled in a mobile sanctuary, at least in metaphor [Ezek. 11:16].) The temple, like the tabernacle, was a physical space where God in his grace *promised* to be accessible to people. We could compare Jesus's promise that "where two or three are gathered in my name, I am there among them" (Matt. 18:20). Because God's presence in this world is most often not evident, his people need such assurances. The temple was a tangible sign of God's gracious accessibility, the earthly footstool of the God who infinitely exceeded it.[7] Of course, like all the ways that God gives us for approaching him, the temple was open to abuse, which the prophets denounced. It could not be a guarantee of divine protection regardless of people's unfaithfulness and disobedience (see Jer. 7:1–11; Mic. 3:9–11). When people did not take seriously, in their behavior, the presence of the holy God among them, God ceased his residence and the palace they had built for him was destroyed.

God's presence was never supposed to be confined to the temple. The image of the temple as God's footstool was one way of making that point.[8] Solomon's prayer at the dedication of the temple made the point emphatically: "Even heaven and the highest heaven cannot contain you, much less this house that I have built!" (1 Kings 8:27). Another way of specifying the limited nature of God's presence in the temple was to speak of it as the place where the Lord's Name dwelled (e.g., Deut. 12:5, 11, 21; 1 Kings 8:29; 14:21). His Name is his personal name, revealed to his people so that they could call him by name (see chap. 2). For God's Name to dwell in the temple means that he is personally present there, specifically in such a way as to

7. 1 Chron. 28:2; Pss. 99:5; 132:7; Lam. 2:1; cf. Isa. 66:1.

8. Similarly, in Isaiah's vision of God in the temple, the mere hem of God's garment fills the temple and his glory fills the whole earth (Isa. 6:1–3).

be accessible to his people's prayers. Thus he says that he has "put [his] name there forever; [his] eyes and [his] heart will be there for all time" (1 Kings 9:3). As the tangible sign of God's accessibility, the temple was not only a place for people to visit but also the place toward which they prayed, wherever they were (1 Kings 8:29–30, 35, 44, 48; Dan. 6:10). The temple enabled all Israelites, however lowly their social status, and even non-Israelites (1 Kings 8:41–43) to meet the God who made and governs the heavens and the earth. Like the descent of the Lord from heaven to be beside Jacob on earth, the temple was a signal form of gracious solidarity with God's people.

The book of Psalms was compiled as the hymnbook of the Second Temple. The individual psalms were composed at many different times and in various circumstances, but many of them were written to be sung or prayed within the temple and some of these evince a strong sense of the nearness of God that the psalmists desired or experienced in the temple. Psalm 84 is an eminent example. It speaks with the voice of someone who presumably lives far from Jerusalem but who makes a pilgrimage to the festivals in the temple whenever possible. He looks forward eagerly to the joy of those times in the near presence of the Lord. He wishes he could be one of those who spend all their time there. Yet he is well aware that it is not mere physical presence in the temple that ensures the Lord's favor and protection. It is on "those who walk uprightly" and "trust in" the Lord that these blessings are bestowed (vv. 11–12). Because the psalmist is one of those people, his intense experience of God in the temple spills over into the rest of his life. He draws strength from God long before he arrives in Jerusalem every few months (vv. 5–7). The psalm is a passionate expression of how the whole of life could be shaped by the divine presence experienced in the temple.

Immanuel

The name Immanuel ("Emmanuel" in the New Testament) means "God (is) with us." It could have been used by Israelite parents to express their gratitude to God for his favor in giving them a child. But its use in Isaiah 7:14 is much more significant than that and constitutes, through the quotation of this verse in Matthew 1:23, one of the most important ways in which the Hebrew Bible's concept of God's "with-ness" is adopted and surpassed in the New Testament.[9]

In its context, Isaiah's reference to a child who will be called Immanuel belongs in a conversation with King Ahaz, the Davidic ruler of Judah at the time. Isaiah has offered Ahaz a sign from God—any sign that Ahaz cared to request—but Ahaz refuses to ask, presumably because he does not believe God's promise (Isa. 7:10–11). In response, Isaiah addresses not only Ahaz himself but also "the house of David" to which Ahaz belongs:

> [13]Hear then, O house of David! Is it too little for you to weary humans, that you weary my God also? [14]Therefore the Lord himself will give you a sign. Look, the young woman is with child and shall bear a son, and shall name him Immanuel. (Isa. 7:13–14 NRSV alt.)

The significance of this "sign" is obscure, as the many interpretations offered by modern scholars show. Who is the young woman? Why is the child called "God-with-us," given that the prophecies that follow are mostly of divine judgment on the house of David?

It is often supposed that when Matthew quotes Isaiah 7:14 (in the Greek version and with some modification) with reference to the birth of Jesus (Matt. 1:22–23), he is detaching the

9. Rev. 21:3 is also very important in this respect.

verse altogether from its context in the Hebrew Bible and from any meaning it could bear in that context. This would not be entirely surprising. Like other early Christians, Matthew would have considered that, of all the books of the Hebrew Bible, Isaiah especially was replete with prophecies of Jesus and his messianic vocation. The mysterious nature of the sign declared by Isaiah in this verse would favor reading it as a prophecy that had been obscure to the prophet himself but was clear now in light of its fulfillment (cf. 1 Pet. 1:10–12).

However, it is arguable that Matthew was quite alert to the literary context of this verse. Isaiah 7 is about the failure of the Davidic dynasty, represented here by King Ahaz. But the name of the child, "God-with-us," recalls how God was "with" David, granting him success in every way, including military success,[10] which Isaiah's oracle goes on to deny to Ahaz and the house of David in the future (Isa. 7:17). It looks as though the "sign," the birth of Immanuel, while ominous for Ahaz and his successors, is essentially a positive expression of hope beyond disaster. God is not with Ahaz, but he is with "us," the faithful remnant of which Isaiah speaks elsewhere (6:13; 8:17). In that case, Immanuel should be seen as a messianic figure, a Davidic king who will represent a new beginning beyond the failure of the dynasty descended through Ahaz. This would be coherent with the image in Isaiah 11:1, where the tree of David's dynasty has been felled, but a new shoot grows from its stump. If Immanuel is a messianic child, then we can see Isaiah 9:6–7 as a much fuller account of his significance.

Matthew's Gospel begins with the genealogy that traces Jesus's descent from Abraham and David (1:1–17). Its main purpose is to establish Jesus's right to the throne of David, as the Messiah of David's line, the new David. Therefore it is

10. 1 Sam. 16:18; 18:12, 14, 28; 2 Sam. 5:10; 7:9; 1 Kings 1:37; 11:38.

immediately followed by Matthew's account of the birth of Jesus into the household of Joseph, a descendant of David. The genealogy traces the line of David through the kings of Judah, including Ahaz, down to the time of the Babylonian exile, when their rule came to an end, as the prophets had predicted, and the surviving members of the royal family were taken into exile. In other words, Matthew here portrays the failure of the Davidic dynasty to which Isaiah 7 alludes. Following the deportation to Babylon, the genealogy lists mostly obscure figures, probably heads of the house of David, monarchs in waiting, from Zerubbabel down to Joseph the father of Jesus.

It is in this context that Matthew then narrates the conception and birth of Jesus (1:18–25), including Isaiah's oracle about Immanuel (1:23). Matthew surely understood it as anticipating a new beginning for David's line beyond the failure of the dynasty in the time of the prophets. Moreover, the meaning of the name Immanuel is important for Matthew. For his readers he gives the Greek translation: "God is with us." In the Greek, as in the Hebrew, there is no verb "is." So the question arises: Does Matthew, like Isaiah, see the child and his name as a sign *that* God is with his people, or does he understand it to mean that Jesus *is* "God-with-us," the human presence of God with his people? It may be that, at this point in the story Matthew tells, the question is left open. But much follows in the Gospel that will incline readers to adopt the second option. We cannot discuss here the many indications in the Gospel that Jesus speaks and acts as one who shares the unique identity of God. Instead we shall focus on the end of the Gospel, which is evidently designed to recall the beginning.

Correspondence between the beginning and the end of a literary unit, with the same themes or words occurring at both ends, is a well-known ancient literary device called *inclusio*, which occurs often in the New Testament. In the case of Matthew's Gospel, the correspondences are between the first two chapters and the last section (28:16–20), which narrates the last appearance of Jesus after the resurrection and his last words in the Gospel. The correspondences are as follows:

1. Jesus is a ruler: he is king of the Jews (2:1–6) and has authority over all things in heaven and earth (28:18);
2. Jesus is the Messiah for the nations as well as for the Jews (1:1[11]; 2:2–11), and the nations are to be baptized "in the name of the Father and of the Son and of the Holy Spirit" (28:19);
3. Jesus is worshiped (2:2, 8, 11; 28:17);[12]
4. Jesus is "God with us" (1:23; 28:20).

In each case, the beginning should be read in the light of the end.

Our focus now is on the last of these correspondences. Jesus's last words, the closing words of the Gospel, are "Behold, I am with you always until the end of the age" (Matt. 28:20 NRSV alt.). The connection with 1:23 is clear, but the difference is highly significant. There Jesus was said to be "God with us"; here he says, "I am with you." God's presence is equated with Jesus's own presence. He speaks *as God*, giving the assurance of divine presence with God's people that throughout the story of Israel had been given by God. Indeed, careful readers of Genesis might well be reminded of God's promise to Jacob at Bethel ("Behold, I am with you," Gen. 28:15 NRSV alt.).

11. The genealogy shows Jesus to be not only the Son of David, the Messiah of Israel, but also the Offspring of Abraham, who is to be a blessing to the nations (Gen. 12:3, etc.).

12. While the verb *proskyneō* need not imply divine worship, careful study of Matthew's usage shows that in his Gospel it does.

This is not the only resemblance between Jacob's dream and the closing section of Matthew's Gospel, especially when we remember that the eleven disciples in Matthew represent the messianically renewed Israel, while Jacob was the ancestor of the people of Israel and was later given the name Israel. In both cases there is promise of continuing presence until the end:

> Behold, I am with you and will keep you wherever you go, and will bring you back to this land; for I will not leave you until I have done what I have promised you. (Gen. 28:15 NRSV alt.)

> Behold, I am with you always until the end of the age. (Matt. 28:20 NRSV alt.)

In both cases God's promise to bless all the nations through the offspring of Abraham is recalled:

> All the families of the earth will be blessed in you and in your offspring. (Gen. 28:14)

> Go therefore and make disciples of all nations. (Matt. 28:19)

The allusions are not such that we can be sure Matthew's first readers were intended to see them. But Matthew's text is certainly open to the identification of the allusions by readers who read them in the context of the whole biblical story. The promise of an accompanying presence of God that would never fail, first given to Jacob, is now renewed and extended, by implication, to the nations that become Jacob's offspring through faith in the Messiah. This happens through a form of the divine presence that Jacob could never have anticipated: the presence of God in the midst of human life *as* the human Jesus, Jacob's own descendant, who thus brings blessing to the nations. Jesus himself is God-with-us.

Jesus as the Staircase in Jacob's Dream

We have seen how the closing section of Matthew's Gospel chimes with Jacob's dream. The New Testament contains one other allusion to Jacob's dream, and in this case the allusion is as clear as we could wish. It occurs in a very significant place: the saying of Jesus in John 1:51. "Amen, amen, I say to you [plural], you will see heaven opened and the angels of God ascending and descending upon the Son of Man" (NRSV alt.).

That this is an explicit allusion to Genesis 28:12 is unmistakable because the words "the angels of God ascending and descending upon" (eight consecutive words in the Greek) correspond exactly to the text of Genesis. This saying constitutes the first teaching Jesus gives in this Gospel, since words of Jesus up to this point have been conversation rather than teaching. It is also the first of twenty-five key sayings of Jesus in this Gospel that are marked out as especially significant by the introduction, "Amen, amen, I say to you" (in most modern versions rendered as "Truly, truly, I say to you" or "Very truly, I say to you"). (This is John's variation on the shorter form used by Jesus in the other Gospels, "Amen, I say to you" ["Truly, I say to you"].)

As if this were not enough to indicate the significance of this saying, we should also note that this is the first saying of ten in John's Gospel in which Jesus refers to himself as "the Son of Man." In this Gospel, Jesus uses this enigmatic form of self-reference when he wishes to speak about his destiny, usually his death-and-exaltation.[13] I use the hyphenated phrase "death-and-exaltation" to refer to John's distinctive view of the cross as simultaneously a physical "lifting up" of Jesus on the

13. The others are 3:13, 14; 5:27; 6:27, 53, 62; 8:28; 12:23; 13:31. (In 12:34 the phrase is used by the crowd.) Of these, only 6:53 has the introduction, "Amen, amen, I say to you."

wood into the air and a symbolic exaltation of Jesus to heavenly glory. It is not accidental that several of these other "Son of Man" sayings refer, as 1:51 does, to movement up and/or down (3:13; 3:14; 6:62; 8:28). Most of them are riddles—deliberately enigmatic sayings that are not understood by the characters in the story but are meant to tease the hearer or reader into thinking about them and discovering their meaning, which becomes clear as the Gospel story proceeds.

The saying that alludes to Jacob's dream is just such a riddle. Though we are not told whether the five men who have only just become followers of Jesus understood it, it is very unlikely that they could have done. They may not even have understood that Jesus was talking about himself. What they are to see is described in visionary language ("you will see heaven opened"), like Jacob's dream-vision. Heaven will be opened, not so that they can see into it (like Stephen in Acts 7:55–56) but so that they can see the angels entering heaven and leaving it, as they pass between heaven and earth.[14] In Jacob's dream, of course, the angels ascend and descend *on the staircase*. The obvious meaning of Jesus's saying is that, in the vision he promises, the angels are to ascend and descend *on the Son of Man*. Many scholars have been reluctant to admit this and have offered more complex understandings of how the saying relates to Jacob's dream. But the obvious correspondence is between the staircase and the Son of Man, while the disciples, who are to see the vision, correspond to Jacob himself. This fits well with the fact that Jesus has just designated Nathanael "truly an Israelite in whom there is no deceit" (John 1:47). By contrast with Jacob, who, when he saw the vision, had just tricked his

14. Similarly, in Jesus's baptismal vision, heaven is opened so that the Spirit can descend to earth (Mark 1:10), and in Peter's vision, heaven is opened so that a sheet can be lowered out of it (Acts 10:11).

brother out of his father's blessing, Nathanael represents the faithful Israel of the last days who will believe in the Messiah. The saying of Jesus in 1:51 is actually addressed in the first place to Nathanael, though its plural "you" shows that the other disciples are also included.

So the disciples, constituting a kind of second Jacob, are to see the angels ascending to heaven and descending from heaven on a staircase constituted by Jesus. In other words, Jesus himself is to be the way across the gap between heaven and earth. But we can be more specific if we compare this saying with later, equally riddling, sayings in which Jesus says that he is going to be "lifted up." For example, in another creative use of a text from the Hebrew Bible, Jesus says, "Just as Moses lifted up the serpent in the wilderness, so must the Son of Man be lifted up, that whoever believes in him may have eternal life" (John 3:14–15).[15] The reference is to the story in Numbers 21:6–9, where Moses lifts up a bronze snake on a pole so that those who have been bitten by poisonous snakes can look at it and escape dying from the poison. In Jesus's saying, "lifting up" is a riddling reference to the cross. Similarly, the saying in John 1:51 depicts Jesus as "lifted up" like a staircase or ladder.[16] The angels probably function only, as they do in Genesis 28:12, to indicate that the staircase/ladder is one that joins heaven to earth.

Jesus, who has come down from heaven, on the cross creates a way to heaven that he takes himself and that those who believe in him can also take: "I, when I am lifted up from the earth, will draw all people to myself" (John 12:32). This is also what Jesus means when he claims to be "the way, and the truth, and the life" (14:6), the way that can be traveled to his Father's

15. For "lifting up" see also John 8:28; 12:32–34.

16. As in the Greek version of Gen. 28:12, the Hebrew word may be seen as referring to a ladder.

house (14:2–3). It is not just that Jesus opens up the way; he is himself the way. Similarly, he is the staircase or ladder between heaven and earth.

In Jacob's dream, as we have seen, the significance of the staircase is not that Jacob must ascend it to reach God in heaven, but that God has descended it in order to be "with" Jacob on earth. Jesus's reinterpretation of the image does not correspond exactly to this meaning. But we should recall that, in John's Gospel, Jesus can only be the way to heaven because he has descended from heaven (3:13; 6:62). He was "with" the disciples on earth (14:9, 25; 17:12) so that they might be "with" him in heavenly glory (17:24; cf. 14:2). This Gospel uses stronger and distinctive language for the divine presence in the lives of the disciples after the resurrection,[17] but the significant little word "with" retains its place in this language (14:17).

Jesus as New Tabernacle and New Temple

Since Jacob, as a result of his dream, identified the place where he experienced the divine presence as "the house of God" (Bethel), John 1:51 has sometimes been taken to evoke the theme of Jesus as the new temple. But there is no allusion to that aspect of the Genesis narrative, and to import it into this context would complicate and obscure the real point of Jesus's saying, which is to take Jacob's ladder as a symbol of his "lifting up" on the cross.

However, the portrayal of Jesus as the new temple—more precisely, the temple of the messianic age foreseen by Ezekiel (Ezek. 40–47) and other prophets—is itself a significant theme in the Gospel of John. Most aspects of it do not relate very

17. See John 14:17, 20, 23; 17:23.

directly to our theme of the divine presence,[18] and so we shall confine our attention here to a key verse in the Prologue to this Gospel:

> And the Word became flesh and dwelled [*eskēnōsen*] among us, and we have seen his glory, glory as of the Only One from the Father, full of grace and truth. (John 1:14 AT)[19]

Some linguistic information will be helpful here. The Greek verb *skēnoō*, which I have translated here as "dwelled," is related to the Greek word for "tent" (*skēnē*), and so it can mean "to live in a tent" or "to encamp." But it can also mean more generally "to take up residence," "to stay" (in the sense of "to live somewhere"). Hence one translation of this verse has "made his home among us" (REB) and another has "lived for a while among us" (NIV), though the implication of *temporary* residence is not necessarily present. But to grasp the full significance of the use of the verb in this verse, we must take account of the fact that this Greek verb resembles the Hebrew verb *šākan* in the sense that it shares the same three consonants (and in a Hebrew word it is the three-consonant root that matters). By a happy linguistic coincidence this Hebrew verb means "to take up residence," "to dwell," a word which the Hebrew Bible uses to refer to God's dwelling in the tabernacle in the wilderness (e.g., Exod. 25:8) or, less often, in the temple on Mount Zion (e.g., Isa. 8:18). In fact, the Hebrew word for "tabernacle" is from the same root (*miškān*), meaning a dwelling place. As we know, it was actually a tent. So the match between the Greek and Hebrew terms is remarkable, and the Greek translators of the Hebrew Bible took advantage of it,

18. E.g., John 7:37–38 alludes to the image of the water of life flowing from the new temple in Ezek. 47:1–12.

19. "AT" will be used to designate author's translation.

sometimes using the compound verb *kataskēnoō* to translate *šākan*, when used of God (e.g., Num. 35:34), and often using *skēnē* to refer to the tabernacle.

With this background it seems certain that the phrase "dwelled among us" in John 1:14 echoes texts where God says, "I the Lord dwell among [you]" (e.g., Num. 35:34), referring to the tabernacle in the wilderness, or, perhaps more relevantly, those where he says, "I will dwell in your midst" (e.g., Zech. 2:10–11), referring to the messianic age. An association with the period in the wilderness is certainly strengthened by the following verses, which refer to the giving of the law to Moses on Mount Sinai and to the occasion on which Moses, on Mount Sinai, asked to see God's glory but was not permitted to see God (i.e., God's face [Exod. 33:18–23]), while the phrase "full of grace and truth" (John 1:14) echoes the way, on the same occasion, God described himself to Moses (Exod. 34:6).[20]

The implication, then, is that the incarnation of the Word ("the Word became flesh") is something analogous to the way God dwelled with his people in the wilderness ("dwelled among us") but surpasses that presence. In Jesus, God's human presence, the unique Son who reflects the glory of his Father, God's essential character ("full of grace and truth") becomes visible, as it was not to Moses. In this unique and novel form of God's presence "with us," the hope of the prophets—that God will in the future dwell in a new temple in the midst of his people—is fulfilled. Jesus himself is God among us, the new tabernacle or temple that fulfills and surpasses those of the Mosaic covenant.

The combination of old and new here is hugely important for understanding how the incarnation is a unique form of the divine presence. The opening words of John 1:14, "the Word

20. See chap. 3 on the divine character.

became flesh," have no precedent at all in the Hebrew Bible. This is astonishingly novel. The word "flesh" in John's Gospel refers to human nature in its weakness and mortality. It emphasizes the difference between human and divine nature (cf. 3:6). The Word, who both "was with God" and "was God," became utterly human. This verse is also the point at which the Prologue transitions from "Word" language to "Son" language. The Word's human presence, *as* the human being Jesus, is fully personal and so can be seen to be the presence of the Son who shares his Father's glory and who, like his Father, is "full of grace and truth."

The strikingly, even shockingly, novel expression "the Word became flesh" is immediately followed by the biblically familiar expression "and dwelled among us." Just as the God revealed in Jesus is the same God, "full of grace and truth," who was known to Moses, so his presence in Jesus is a "being with" his people, a "dwelling among them," as it was in the earliest days of Israel's history, when they were constituted his people in part by that very fact. But while God's "being with" humans is in any case something remarkable, incarnation, in which God comes to be with us actually as one of us, a fellow human, surpasses any possible expectation. The Prologue to John presents this to us so that we may then read the Gospel's story as the story of "God with us" in this most profound sense.

God with Us in the End

The theme of divine "with-ness," which we have traced from Genesis onward, goes with us as far as the end of the Bible: the book of Revelation's vision of the new creation and the New Jerusalem. When God brings to fulfillment and perfection his whole history with the world, this will be the essential relationship of humans with God forever:

> Behold, the dwelling place [or tabernacle: *skēnē*] of God is with humans, and he will dwell [*skēnōsei*] with them, and they will be his peoples, and God himself will be with them. (Rev. 21:3b AT)[21]

The threefold repetition of "with" makes this one of the most emphatic statements of divine "with-ness" in Scripture.

As in much of Revelation, prophecies from the Hebrew Bible are here being reprised, brought together and interpreted. The divine promises from the Hebrew Bible that underlie this passage are these:

> [26b][I] will set my sanctuary [*miqdāš*] among them [Israel] forevermore. [27]My dwelling place [*miškān*] shall be with them; and I shall be their God, and they shall be my people. (Ezek. 37:26b–27)

> [10b]For lo, I will come and dwell in your midst, says the Lord. [11]Many nations shall join themselves to the Lord on that day, and shall be my peoples; and I will dwell [*šākan*] in your midst. (Zech. 2:10b–11a [Heb. 2:14b–15a])

These passages both use the Hebrew terminology for God's dwelling in the tabernacle and the temple, and we can see how Revelation 21:3 has picked this up with the equivalent terms in Greek. Also noteworthy is the way Ezekiel's focus on Israel ("my people") is expanded in Zechariah to include the "many nations" who, in the messianic age, will become God's

21. Some manuscripts have "people" and this reading is reflected in some English translations, but the better reading is certainly "peoples."

"peoples." This too is picked up in Revelation, so that for the first time God's "with-ness" presence becomes a universal presence, not just with his singular people Israel and not just with the new people the church, but with "humans" who become God's "peoples."

All the blessings of eternal life follow from this perfected divine "with-ness." Here we shall note only the one that immediately follows the passage just quoted: God "will wipe every tear from their eyes" (Rev. 21:4a). The promise comes almost word for word from Isaiah 25:8. It evokes unforgettably the loving intimacy of the divine presence with humans in the new creation. The abolition of death and suffering (Rev. 21:4b) is not just a metaphysical act of the omnipotent God; it is the fruit of the communion between God and humans. In their common life together, the divine compassion and the life of the ever-living God ensure that sorrow and death can never again intrude.

Reflecting on this passage in connection with our exposition of John 1:14, we might wonder what has become of the incarnation. In John 1:14 the prophetic hopes of God's dwelling with his people are fulfilled in Jesus, the new tabernacle, whereas in Revelation 21:3 there is talk only of God himself dwelling with his peoples. But as we read on, we learn that Jesus Christ is far from absent from the New Jerusalem. The prophet says, "I saw no temple in the city, for its temple is the Lord God the Almighty and the Lamb" (Rev. 21:22). In one sense, the whole city is a temple, because it takes the form of a perfect cube (21:16), the shape of the holy of holies in the temple, where God was present. In another sense, the city has no temple, because it, like the holy of holies, is entirely filled with the divine presence. So, instead of a special place where God was present, "the Lord God the Almighty and the Lamb" are the temple.

Bibliographic Notes

On Divine Presence

Samuel Terrien, *The Elusive Presence: Toward a New Biblical Theology* (San Francisco: Harper & Row, 1978).

Ingolf U. Dalferth, *Becoming Present: An Inquiry into the Christian Sense of the Presence of God*, Studies in Philosophical Theology 30 (Leuven: Peeters, 2006).

David D. Kupp, *Matthew's Emmanuel: Divine Presence and God's People in the First Gospel*, Society for New Testament Studies Monograph Series 90 (Cambridge: Cambridge University Press, 1996). (As well as a study of Matthew, this book includes a survey of the Old Testament material.)

On the Tabernacle and the Temple

Gregory K. Beale, *The Temple and the Church's Mission: A Biblical Theology of the Dwelling Place of God*, New Studies in Biblical Theology (Leicester: Apollos, 2005).

Philip P. Jenson, *Graded Holiness: A Key to the Priestly Conception of the World*, Journal for the Study of the Old Testament Supplement Series 106 (Sheffield: Sheffield Academic, 1992).

On Immanuel in Matthew

Richard B. Hays, *Echoes of Scripture in the Gospels* (Waco: Baylor University Press, 2016), 139–74.

On John 1:51

Richard Bauckham, *Gospel of Glory: Major Themes in Johannine Theology* (Grand Rapids: Baker Academic, 2015), 166–80.

On Temple Imagery in John

Mary L. Coloe, *God Dwells with Us: Temple Symbolism in the Fourth Gospel* (Collegeville, MN: Liturgical Press, 2001).

Paul M. Hoskins, *Jesus as the Fulfillment of the Temple in the Gospel of John*, Paternoster Biblical Monographs (Milton Keynes, UK: Paternoster, 2006).

On Revelation 21

Richard Bauckham, *The Theology of the Book of Revelation* (Cambridge: Cambridge University Press, 1993), 136–43.

2

The Revelation of the Divine Name

Representing the Divine Name

By way of preface to the subject of this chapter, some readers may need a word of explanation about the way the Hebrew name of God is represented in print. The Name consists of the four Hebrew letters YHWH (*yōd*, *hē*, *wāw*, *hē*). The Name is sometimes known as the Tetragrammaton, which means "four letters." For reasons we shall note later in this chapter, sometime in the period of Jewish history between the Babylonian exile and the time of Jesus, Jews stopped pronouncing the Name and adopted substitutes that they spoke when reading the Scriptures where the Name occurred. Although some—not entirely consistent—evidence has survived as to how the Name was pronounced, we cannot really be sure of the pronunciation of it in ancient Israel. In the ancient period, Hebrew vowels were not written. Much later, vowel points (marks indicating the vowels) were added in manuscripts of the Hebrew Bible, but in the case of the Divine Name the vowels that were added were not those that once belonged to the Name itself but those of the Hebrew word that was generally used as a substitute for the Name when reading the Bible: *ʾădōnāy*, which means "my Lord." In the Hebrew Bible, therefore, the Divine Name is not pronounceable.

Most English translations of the Old Testament respect and continue the Jewish practice of using a substitute for the Name. In those versions the Name is represented in English by "the LORD." The use of four uppercase letters (LORD) indicates that in these cases the English word is a substitute for the Tetragrammaton, which is not the case where God is called "the Lord." (Sometimes, in the Hebrew Bible, God is called "the Lord YHWH." In these cases the English versions have "the Lord GOD.")

Jesus and the early Christians followed the Jewish practice of not speaking the Divine Name but using a substitute instead. (In Greek this was usually *kyrios*, "Lord." This will be discussed further below.) In my view, this is a good reason for Christians to do the same. Accordingly, while I sometimes represent the Name by the four Hebrew letters YHWH, without vocalization, in this chapter I usually follow the practice of English translations and render the Name as "the LORD."

The Burning Bush

The disclosure of the Divine Name is recounted in the story of Moses and the burning bush (Exod. 3). At this point in the biblical narrative, Moses has had to leave Egypt and has become a shepherd, working for his father-in-law:

> 1Moses was keeping the flock of his father-in-law Jethro, the
> priest of Midian; he led his flock beyond the wilderness, and

> came to Horeb, the mountain of God. [2]There the angel of the Lord appeared to him in a flame of fire out of a bush; he looked, and the bush was blazing, yet it was not consumed. [3]Then Moses said, "I must turn aside and look at this great sight, and see why the bush is not burned up." [4]When the Lord saw that he had turned aside to see, God called to him out of the bush, "Moses, Moses!" And he said, "Here I am." [5]Then he said, "Come no closer! Remove the sandals from your feet, for the place on which you are standing is holy ground." [6]He said further, "I am the God of your father, the God of Abraham, the God of Isaac, and the God of Jacob." And Moses hid his face, for he was afraid to look at God. (Exod. 3:1–6)

In comparison with the many other encounters with God that the Hebrew Bible relates, this one has some remarkable features. That it is "the Angel of the Lord" who appears to Moses is not unusual. Frequently in the early books of the Bible, when the figure of the Angel of the Lord appears, this angel is not just a messenger of God, like most angels, but virtually the presence of God himself on earth.[1] The angel's presence is God's presence; what the angel says, God says. However, what is remarkable in this case is the way the angel appears: as a flame of fire in a bush. The bush is blazing. It looks as though it is on fire, but the fire does not consume it. There is nothing at all like this in the rest of the Bible. It is a unique form of theophany.

Another unusual feature is that Moses is told to remove his sandals because the ground is holy. No doubt this means that the holy presence of God renders the ground holy. This is striking especially because, if one were reading through the Bible from the beginning, this is the first time one would encounter the word "holy." The words "holy" and "holiness" do not appear

1. E.g., Gen. 16:7–14; 22:9–19; Judg. 6:11–24; 13:2–23.

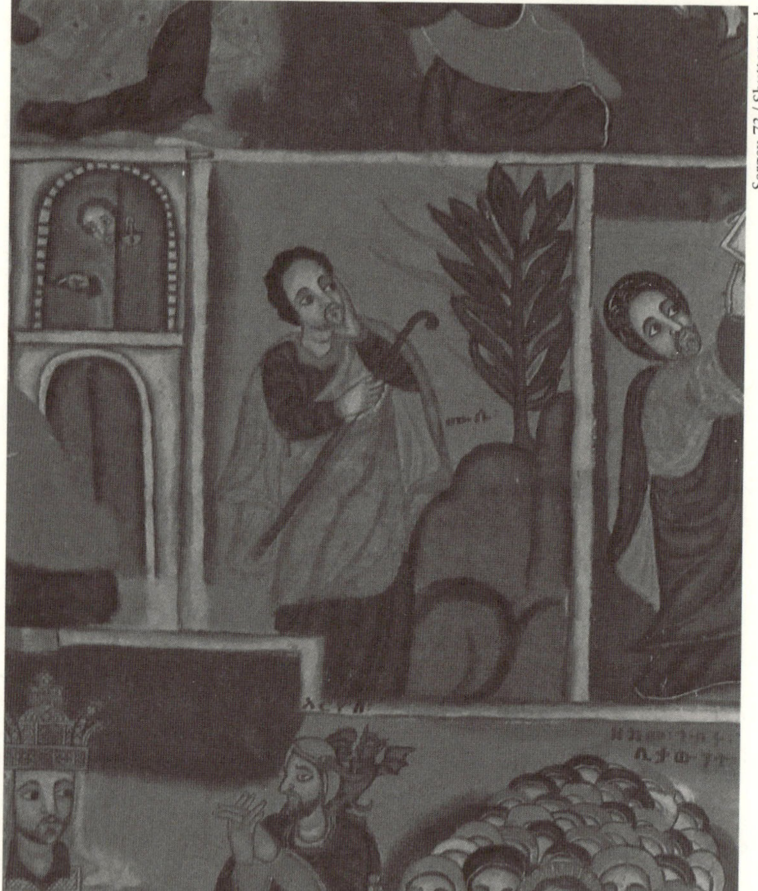

Figure 2. Moses and the Burning Bush. Monastery on an island near Lake Tana, Ethiopia

in Genesis.[2] But, starting from Exodus 3:5, these words appear frequently in the rest of the Pentateuch. This may be an indication that God's special relationship with his people Israel, the people made holy by God's presence among them, begins here.

The point is reinforced by the way that Moses is required to acknowledge the holiness of God's presence. On only one

2. The related verb "to make holy," "to hallow" appears in Gen. 2:3.

other occasion in the Bible is someone told to remove their shoes because the ground is holy—when the Commander of the heavenly army appears to Joshua (Josh. 5:15). Probably, the Israelites went barefoot when they entered the tabernacle and the temple, but we are never actually told that in the Old Testament. It was a common custom in the ancient Near East (continued today by Muslims, who take off their shoes when they enter mosques) and may well be taken for granted in the biblical accounts of the temple. But the Hebrew Bible never directs attention to it. No commandment requires it. So it is very striking that here in Exodus 3 the Angel of the Lord tells Moses to remove his sandals because the ground is holy. Here begins, as it were, the story of God's holy presence with his people.

The final noteworthy feature of this passage is that God introduces himself to Moses as "the God of your father, the God of Abraham, the God of Isaac, and the God of Jacob." Although he had not appeared to the patriarchs in this way, in a flaming fire, there is no doubt that he is the same God who called Abraham and made his still unfulfilled promises to the ancestors of the people of Israel.

In the following verses, God goes on to tell Moses that he has observed the miserable circumstances of the people of Israel in Egypt and has heard their prayers imploring his help. The people, and Moses himself, might well have supposed that the God of their fathers had forgotten them, or even disowned them. But God assures Moses that this is not the case. He intends to free the people from Egypt and give them the land of Canaan. Moses is to be his agent. At this Moses protests:

> [11]But Moses said to God, "Who am I that I should go to Pharaoh, and bring the Israelites out of Egypt?" [12]He [God] said, "I will be with you; and this shall be the sign for you that it is I who

> sent you: when you have brought the people out of Egypt, you shall worship God on this mountain." (Exod. 3:11–12)

But Moses is not satisfied with this assurance:

> Moses said to God, "If I come to the Israelites and say to them, 'The God of your ancestors has sent me to you,' and they ask me, 'What is his name?' what shall I say to them?" (3:13)

Why should the Israelites need to know the name of their ancestors' God? Why is it not enough to know that he is the God of their forefathers, Abraham, Isaac, and Jacob? The most obvious reason is that they live in a world in which gods have names. All around them in Egypt live people who invoke the Egyptian gods—Ra, Osiris, Isis, Horus, Set, and others. To call on one of these gods for favor, one had to distinguish one from another by their names. Gods were no use unless one could call on them by name. There may even have been the sense that to know a god's name was to have some power to make the god respond. So if the God who sent Moses was really going to help the Israelites, they needed a name with which to call on him.

So Moses asks what name he can give them. God's answers to this question are the focus of our interest in this chapter. In fact, God answers Moses three times or in three stages:

> 14God said to Moses, "**I will be who I will be.**"
>
> He said further, "Thus you shall say to the Israelites, '**I-Will-Be** has sent me to you.'"
>
> 15God also said to Moses, "Thus you shall say to the Israelites, '**The Lord**, the God of your ancestors, the God of Abraham, the God of Isaac, and the God of Jacob, has sent me to you':

> This is my name forever,
> and this is my appellation for all generations.
>
> [16]Go and assemble the elders of Israel, and say to them, "The Lord, the God of your ancestors, the God of Abraham, of Isaac, and of Jacob, has appeared to me, saying: 'I have given heed to you and to what has been done to you in Egypt.'" (Exod. 3:14–16 NRSV alt.)

The writer has set out God's answer in three carefully marked stages: "God said," "he said further," "God also said." The three distinct introductions to God's words give a certain solemnity to the account, but they also distinguish three stages in God's answer. Each of the three stages should be taken seriously in its own right. Then we will be able to take full account of the fact that only at the third stage does God actually gives Moses what he asked for—a name.

God's first answer to Moses certainly does not provide a name. On the contrary, it looks very much like a refusal to give a name. It consists of three Hebrew words: *ʾehyeh*, *ʾăšer*, and *ʾehyeh*.

What exactly is meant has been much debated, partly because the Hebrew verbs can have either a present or a future meaning. The translation could be either "I am who I am" or "I will be who I will be."[3] Most of the English versions of the Bible opt for "I am who I am," which is probably how the words have most often been understood in the past. But the majority of scholars now probably favor the future meaning: "I will be who I will be." One reason is that the context concerns what God is going to do: he is going to send Moses and deliver the

3. Another possible translation is "I am the one who is." This is how the Greek (LXX) version of the Old Testament rendered it. Consequently, this interpretation has been very influential in the Christian theological tradition.

people. In fact, God has already, in his answer to Moses's first question, used the word *ʾehyeh* with future meaning: "I will be with you" (Exod. 3:12).

A second reason for preferring a future meaning is that parallels to the particular linguistic construction used here suggest an idiom that has future reference. For example, in Exodus 16:23, God tells the Israelites what to do with the manna. Literally what he says is: "Bake what you will bake and boil what you will boil." The meaning is: "Bake as much as you want to bake and boil as much as you want to boil" (AT). Another example is in Ezekiel 12:25, where God says, "I the Lord will speak the word that I will speak, and it will be fulfilled" (NRSV alt.). The meaning is something like, "I will say whatever I choose to say" or "I will say whatever I decide to say." The idiom is about having and making a free choice. So what God says to Moses amounts to: "I will be whoever I choose to be" or "I am free to be who I choose to be."

In more technical language, we might say that God is utterly self-determining. He cannot be constrained by anything other than himself. He can say who he is and who he will be only by reference to himself, not by reference to anything else. God is who he chooses to be. Another reason I am convinced of this interpretation is that it coheres with the symbolism of the burning bush. The fire blazes but does not consume the bush. Any other fire needs to consume fuel. It can only continue to blaze while there is stuff it can consume. Then it goes out. But the fire in the bush is self-sustaining. It needs no fuel. It blazes as it chooses. Similarly, God is self-subsistent and self-determining. He will be who he chooses to be.

So it sounds as though, in God's first response to Moses, he is refusing to be named. A name would tie him down. It would put him at the beck and call of anyone who knows his name. Names define and limit and constrain. If the reason the Israelites want to know their God's name is so that they can call him to their aid like some genie in a lamp, then he will not be named. But we should notice that God has in fact, in this narrative, already told Moses something about what he will be: "I will be with you" (Exod. 3:12). So God, in his free self-determination, can and does commit himself. He gives promises that he will keep. The point is that God commits *himself*.

This explains how God then moves to the second stage of his answer to Moses: "Thus you shall say to the Israelites, 'I-Will-Be has sent me to you'" (Exod. 3:14b). Here God abbreviates his self-declaration, "I will be who I will be." He condenses the three words (*ʾehyeh ʾăšer ʾehyeh*) into one word (*ʾehyeh*). And he uses that one word—utterly ungrammatically—as though it were a name. Moses is to say, "I-Will-Be has sent me." It means that the One who cannot be *constrained*, even by Israel's cries for help, *commits himself* to a course of action for Israel's sake. The self-determining One determines himself to be Israel's Savior, the One who is sending Moses to deliver the people. By using the statement of his freedom to be who he chooses in the way he does here, making it function like a name in a statement of commitment, God declares himself to be the God who himself has chosen, in his grace and his love, to be Israel's God, dedicated to Israel's good. This is a name that expresses his loving commitment to Israel but cannot be used to constrain or control him.

Only now, at the third stage of his answer to Moses, does God give himself a real name: "Thus you shall say to the Israelites, 'The Lord [YHWH], the God of your ancestors, the God of Abraham, the God of Isaac, and the God of Jacob, has sent me to you'" (Exod. 3:15a). The name YHWH looks like the verb *ʾehyeh*, and even without the vowels we can tell that it would sound rather like *ʾehyeh*. Three of its four letters (*yōd*, *hē*, *wāw*, *hē*) are found in the word *ʾehyeh* (*hē*, *yōd*, *hē*), and so it looks as though it ought to be another form of the verb "to be" (the verb *hāyāh*). Some scholars argue that it is—that it means "he is" or "he will be"—although this form is not actually attested in extant Hebrew. But this is no more than a conjecture. We do not really know what the Divine Name means, if it means anything in the ordinary sense. What seems much clearer is that there is a *play on words* between *ʾehyeh* and YHWH. This is common in the Bible when a personal name is explained. When a child is named and an explanation is given, very often the explanation is not a true etymology of the name but a play on words. The name is explained by a word that sounds rather like it.[4] What matters in God's dialogue with Moses is not the etymology of the Name, but that God first uses "I-will-be" as though it were a name and then associates his personal Name with that usage by means of a play on words.

So the two stages of God's answer to Moses that precede the giving of his actual, personal Name make it clear what is expressed in the giving of the Name: it does not negate God's self-determination. It does not reduce him to being Israel's God, a god who serves Israel's purposes, a tribal demi-god. But it does mean that, in his grace, in the freedom of his love, God has committed himself to Israel, chosen to be Israel's God—and has done so, it seems, irrevocably: "This is my name forever, and this is my appellation for all generations" (Exod. 3:15b). Giving himself a name means that the people of Israel can call him by name—not that they can control him but that they can *address* him. They can appeal to his love and his loyalty. The

4. E.g., Gen. 4:1; 25:26; 29:32, 33, 34, 35; 30:8, 18, 20. This is especially the case in Genesis, since the true etymology of these archaic names was probably not known in later times.

Name creates a relationship in which he will be their God and they will be his people. So although the Name is given specifically at this juncture of history, where God commits himself to the exodus, to becoming known as the God who brought the Israelites out of Egypt, the Name also looks forward to all the consequent history of Israel's relationship with this god, Israel's God.

In the rest of the Hebrew Bible the Divine Name occurs more than 6,800 times. It has plausibly been said to constitute the center of Old Testament theology. The huge importance of the Name lies not in any meaning the word itself is supposed to have but in the fact that it stands for the identity of the God who bears it. This is what personal names do. They identify someone and point to all that we know about that person. They sum up who a person is as far as we know that. In God's case, all that God is cannot be known to finite creatures. God remains the infinite mystery that we cannot sum up or pin down. But we can know the particular identity that God has given himself within the world so that people may know and relate to him. His Name names that identity. The revelation of the Name is a supreme act of God's grace, making himself accessible and knowable, making himself Israel's God.

A Name of God for All People?

This raises the question: Is the Divine Name that was revealed to Moses a Name that is only for Israel's use? Christians have often thought so. But we need to remember that God did not make himself Israel's God *for the sake of Israel alone*. He became Israel's God in order, thereby, to make himself the God of all nations. Especially in the prophets we find the expectation growing that, in a great future act of salvation for his people,

God will demonstrate his deity, so that his people Israel will know that he is indeed the LORD and also so that all the nations will recognize Israel's God as the one and only God and worship him themselves. One of the latest of the prophets puts it like this: "And the LORD will become king over all the earth; on that day the LORD will be one and his name one" (Zech. 14:9). He goes on to describe the nations going up to the temple in Jerusalem to worship the LORD there (14:16–19).

That rather arresting prophecy, "The LORD will be one and his name one," is an echo of Israel's confession of faith, the Shema: "The LORD our God, the LORD is one" (Deut. 6:4).[5] Israel came to believe that their God was the one and only true God, Creator of the world and rightful Ruler of the nations. When the prophet says "the LORD will be one," he means that all people will acknowledge that Israel's God, the LORD, is the one and only God of all the earth. It is especially notable that he also says that the LORD's *Name* will be one. The nations will not continue to use the many different names of their gods. They will know God by the one personal Name that identifies him as Israel's God and also as God of all nations.

Christians believe that such promises were fulfilled and are being fulfilled through Jesus Christ. So we should surely expect the New Testament to refer to the personal Name of God. The New Testament writers make it abundantly clear that the God of Jesus, the God of Christian faith, the God of Jewish and Gentile believers alike, is Israel's God, the God who revealed his Name to Israel. The Christian God is not a new god but the same God who spoke to Moses. So what becomes of the Hebrew Divine Name in the New Testament?

5. For this translation see the NRSV margin. It is certainly the way the Shema was understood in the late Second Temple period (the time of Jesus).

Not Speaking the Name

Before answering that question, we need to give a little more attention to the Jewish practice of not pronouncing the Name, since this practice was followed by Jesus and his apostles and all the New Testament writers. By the time of Jesus, most Jews had come to believe that the Divine Name should not be pronounced, except in the temple once a year on the day of atonement, when the high priest pronounced the priestly blessing on the people.[6]

We do not know for sure when or why the idea became dominant that the Divine Name should not normally be spoken. There are indications within the Hebrew Bible itself that the practice of avoiding speaking the Name was already affecting the composition of some of the biblical writings.[7] The most plausible explanation is that the third of the Ten Commandments had a strong influence: "You shall not make wrongful use of the name of the LORD your God, for the LORD will not acquit anyone who misuses his name" (Exod. 20:7; Deut. 5:11). There is no doubt that this commandment especially forbids the careless or dishonest use of oaths sworn in the name of God, but it could also be taken to oppose the use of the Name in magic (since in the ancient world all kinds of divine names were treated as having magical power) or simply in profane ways that showed no reverence for the God whose name it was. Keeping the Name secret protected it from such abuses, and, once the practice of not speaking the Name was common, it would have become a way of generally expressing reverence for God. His Name was holy, and only the high priest within

6. It is possible that the high priest also pronounced the Name when giving the priestly blessing in the temple at other times.

7. E.g., the so-called Elohistic Psalms (Pss. 42–83), where the name YHWH is only occasionally used and God is predominantly called *ʾĕlōhîm* (God).

the holy confines of the sanctuary, his own holiness carefully ensured, was sufficiently holy to speak the holy Name.

However, we need to notice carefully that, while Jews in the time of Jesus generally did not speak the Name, they frequently referred to it. When they read the Scriptures, where the Name constantly appears, they made use of recognized substitutes for the Name. Most often, these seem to have been, in Hebrew, *ʾădōnāy* and, in Greek, *kyrios*. Both words mean "Lord," but they are not translations of the Name, which was never supposed to *mean* "Lord." Rather these words were substitutes, signaling to the reader and the hearers alike that the Tetragrammaton occurred there in the text. These substitutes were not only used when reading Scripture; they were also used by authors writing Jewish literature. Moreover, when Jews prayed, they most commonly addressed God as "Lord," not just as a way of alluding to God's lordship, speaking as a servant to his Lord, but also as a way of referring reverently to the Divine Name. The Name had been given to Israel precisely to enable them to call on him by name. In this later period Jews continued to "call on the name of the LORD" by using the substitutes. We should certainly not suppose that the Name was forgotten or neglected.

The peculiar feature of Jewish practice is that, while the Name was generally unspoken, it was a very frequent subject of reference. The Divine Name was marked out from all other names as unique by this practice of referring to it but not speaking it. Whereas in Gentile religious practice at the time not only were there many gods but also many names of gods were treated as interchangeable, Jews guarded the uniqueness of God's Name by not speaking it. Not only was it different from and not to be used interchangeably with the names of the pagan gods. It was also incomparable, in a class of its own.

(Later the rabbis used the word *ha-Shem*, meaning "the Name," as a substitute for the Tetragrammaton, as some Jews still do.)

In general, the New Testament writings are coherent with this Jewish practice. Usually, when the word *kyrios* appears in quotations from the Old Testament, the word stands for the Divine Name. As we shall see, there are also explicit references to the Divine Name.

Jesus and the Divine Name

There is one reference to the Divine Name in the teaching of Jesus that is very familiar indeed to most Christians: "Hallowed be your name" is the first petition of the Lord's Prayer in both the shorter version in Luke's Gospel (Luke 11:2) and the more familiar, longer version in Matthew (Matt. 6:9). The word "hallowed" is archaic English, and it is somewhat surprising that most modern English versions of the New Testament retain it. They tend to be linguistically conservative when it comes to usages that are as familiar to English-speaking Christians as this. But anyone relying on what the word "hallowed" means when it occasionally appears in modern English would be misled. In the Lord's Prayer, it is the passive of the verb "to hallow," meaning "to treat as holy" or "to sanctify." What the prayer says is: "May your Name be sanctified."

Probably, to many Christians who use the words of this prayer regularly, it does not occur that the name to which Jesus referred is the Hebrew personal Name of God that was revealed to Moses. They may take it as simply a metaphorical way of referring to God, so that the sense of the prayer is: "May God be honored and reverenced." It is true that God's "name" in Scripture can refer to God's reputation or can be virtually a way of referring to God himself, but no Jewish hearer of the

Lord's Prayer in the time of Jesus would imagine that the Name itself was *not* being referenced. In the Psalms "Praise the name of the LORD"[8] does mean "praise God," but it refers to God as the one who is identified by his personal Name. The Name names God's identity. So in the Lord's Prayer, the hallowing of God's Name means the reverent acknowledgment of the holy God whose Name is the Tetragrammaton.

Compare this passage from the prophets:

> 22Therefore say to the house of Israel, Thus says the Lord GOD: It is not for your sake, O house of Israel, that I am about to act, but for the sake of my holy name, which you have profaned among the nations to which you came. 23I will sanctify my great name, which has been profaned among the nations, and which you have profaned among them; and the nations shall know that I am the LORD, says the Lord GOD, when through you I display my holiness before their eyes. (Ezek. 36:22–23)

"I will sanctify my great name": that is precisely what Jesus's prayer is asking God to do. "Your Name be hallowed" is not a mere wish that people will sanctify God's name. It is a prayer requesting God to sanctify his Name, to bring it about that people acknowledge and reverence him. It longs for that great act of salvation by which, the prophets expected, God would make himself known.

In Jesus's prayer, the first petition, "your name be hallowed," stands parallel to "your kingdom come" and, in Matthew's version, "your will be done." Matthew's version adds, qualifying all three petitions, "as in heaven so on earth" (AT). In heaven, God's Name is acknowledged, his rule is obeyed, and his will is done. We pray for God to bring about the same—all

8. E.g., Pss. 69:30; 99:3; 113:3.

three aspects of this world's proper relationship to God—on earth too.

It is worth also comparing this traditional Jewish prayer:

> Exalted and hallowed be his great Name
> in the world he created
> according to his will.
> May he establish his kingdom
> in your lifetime and in your days,
> and in the lifetime of the whole household of Israel,
> speedily and at a near time.[9]

This version of the Qaddish is very much later than the New Testament, but it is a reasonable guess that something like this form of words goes back to the time of Jesus. The hope Jesus expressed in his prayer was essentially no different from the hope his Jewish compatriots and contemporaries regularly expressed in prayer. They would, without question, understand the Name of God to which Jesus refers to be the Name revealed to Moses.

After that it comes as a surprise to find that, in the words of Jesus in the Gospels and leaving aside quotations from the Hebrew Bible, Jesus never refers to God as "Lord," the standard substitute for the Tetragrammaton (except in just two anomalous instances where we must attribute the word to the evangelist[10]). This is a remarkably consistent feature of the words of Jesus. Given the frequency of the use of "Lord" in

9. This translation is by Jakob J. Petuchowski in *The Lord's Prayer and Jewish Liturgy*, ed. Jakob J. Petuchowski and Michael Brocke (London: Burns & Oates, 1978), 37.

10. Mark 5:19; 13:20. Compare the parallels (without "Lord"): Luke 8:39; Matt. 24:22. In the phrases "Lord of heaven and earth" (Matt. 11:25; Luke 10:21) and "the Lord of the harvest" (Matt. 9:38; Luke 10:2), the word "Lord" cannot be a substitute for the Tetragrammaton.

other Jewish literature, it makes Jesus's usage, so far as I am aware, highly unusual or even unique.

So how did Jesus refer to God? One way was the use of what is called the "divine passive." The easiest way to explain this is to give some examples:

> Matthew 5:4: Blessed are those who mourn, for *they will be comforted* (= *God will comfort them*)
>
> Matthew 23:37a: Jerusalem, Jerusalem, the city that kills the prophets and stones *those who are sent to it*! (= *those God sends to it*)
>
> Mark 10:40: To sit at my right hand or at my left is not mine to grant, but it is *for those for whom it has been prepared* (= *for those for whom God has prepared it*)

The divine passive is a way of speaking that attributes an action to God without directly saying so. Instead of saying "God does *x*," one says "*x* is done." This is a Jewish way of speaking that is found in Jewish literature, but Jesus seems to have especially favored it. Sometimes scholars say that it is a way of avoiding using the Divine Name, but one can easily avoid the Divine Name by saying "God" or "the Lord." What the divine passive does is protect God's transcendence. It avoids making God directly the subject of an action in this world.

But Jesus did not and could not speak of God only by use of the divine passive. Quite often he simply uses the word "God" (*theos* in our Greek Gospels). This is a normal Jewish way of speaking. In the Hebrew Bible, God is often called "God" (*ʾĕlōhîm*), though far less often than he is called by the Divine Name. In the later books of the Hebrew Bible and in subsequent Jewish literature, there is a tendency to use "God" more often and the Divine Name less often. However, we need to remember that Jesus usually spoke Aramaic, not Hebrew. So we need to consider how the Divine Name was treated in Jewish Aramaic at this time.[11] Unfortunately, we do not have very much Jewish Aramaic literature from this period, but it seems that in Aramaic Jews did not use the term "Lord" (in Aramaic *Mara'*) as a substitute for the Tetragrammaton. The word *Mara'*—or *Mari*, "my Lord"—is used of God and in address to God, but it is not substituted for the Divine Name. For that purpose Aramaic writers simply used the Aramaic word for God (*'elah*).

So this may, in part, explain Jesus's usage. For example, one of the most frequent phrases Jesus uses for a key topic of his teaching is "the kingdom of God." In Hebrew one would expect that to be "the kingdom of the LORD (YHWH)." The term that appears in our Greek Gospels presumably indicates that Jesus, speaking Aramaic, said "the kingdom of God," using "God" as a substitute for the Divine Name. However, I do not think that use of "God" as a substitute for the Divine Name sufficiently explains Jesus's non-use of "Lord." He did not just use "God" instead. Another characteristic of Jesus's way of speaking of God is his use of the word "Father." In fact, this is the way of referring to God that is most characteristic of Jesus. While Jews in this period did occasionally call God "Father," it was rare. Jesus, on the other hand, seems to have privileged this word for God.[12]

Of most interest is the way Jesus addresses God in prayer. According to the Gospels Jesus *always* addressed God as "Father." The single exception is his cry from the cross, "My God, my God, why have you forsaken me?"[13] in which he adopts the

11. The Aramaic Targums are of considerably later dates.

12. The Gospels have "Father," referring to God, in the words of Jesus as follows: 4 times in Mark, 17 times in Luke, 43 times in Matthew, and 109 times in John.

13. Matt. 27:46; Mark 15:34.

words of Psalm 22:1. In every other case—fifteen times (not counting parallels)—the Gospels represent Jesus as praying to God as "Father."[14] In addition there is the prayer he gave to the disciples for their regular use, which begins simply "Father" in Luke's version (11:2) and "Our Father in heaven" in Matthew's version (6:9). This almost exclusive use of "Father" to address God was certainly very unusual,[15] and the New Testament shows that it was regarded as special and distinctive by preserving the actual Aramaic word Jesus used: Abba. Not only does Mark in his Gospel preserve the Aramaic word "Abba" when he records Jesus's prayer in Gethsemane (14:36), but also Paul refers to Christians praying, "Abba, Father" (Rom. 8:15; Gal. 4:6). He does so in letters written in Greek to Christians in Rome and Galatia, most of whom did not speak Aramaic. For early Christians to have continued to use this word even in contexts where Aramaic was not the local language, they must have thought there was something very special about Jesus's use of this word "Abba" in prayer.

I think these features of Jesus's ways of referring to God must mean that Jesus used the word "Father" as his own chosen substitute for the Divine Name. I am not aware that anyone else has suggested this, but it seems to me to make very good sense of his usage. The Divine Name was revealed to Israel, especially so that God's people could address him by name—"call on the name of the Lord." Whereas Jews in Jesus's time standardly addressed God as "Lord" in Hebrew or as "my God" or "our God" in Aramaic (using these terms as substitutes

14. Matt. 11:25, 26 (Luke 10:21); Matt. 26:39, 42 (Mark 14:36; Luke 22:42); Luke 23:34, 46; John 11:41; 12:27, 28; 17:1, 5, 11, 21, 24, 25. (The references in parentheses are parallel passages.)

15. The only examples of address to God as "Father" in Second Temple period Jewish literature are: Sir. 23:1, 4 (Greek); Wis. 14:3; 3 Macc. 6:2–15; 4Q372 1:1:16; 4Q460 5:1:5; Apocryphon of Ezekiel (quoted in 1 Clem. 8:3); cf. Sir. 51:10 (Hebrew).

for the Name), Jesus chose instead to use "Father." This is Jesus's substitute for the Name, not in the sense of replacing the Name, but in the sense of referring to the Name while not actually speaking it. It is a novel means of reverent reference to the Name. The reason(s) why Jesus did this deserve discussion at length, which would not be appropriate here. But, briefly, the essential reason must be that Jesus was aware of a special relationship with God that he enjoyed as God's Son and that he also shared with others.

When Christians say the Lord's Prayer, addressing God as "Father" and asking God to "hallow" his Name, they are continuing this usage that Jesus innovated: using "Father" as a substitute for the Divine Name, which at the same time refers to the Divine Name.

Jesus the Lord

The New Testament writers use the Greek word "Lord" (*kyrios*) only very occasionally of God, except in Old Testament quotations, where it occurs as the regular substitute for the Divine Name. Usually they call God either "God" or "Father," along with the variations "our Father" and "the Father of Jesus Christ." This looks like a continuation of Jesus's usage, but in another respect their usage is quite different from Jesus's. They use the word "Lord" (*kyrios*) frequently, but with reference to Jesus himself. So, for example, Paul in the opening greetings of his letters uses a standard formula: "Grace to you and peace from God our Father and the Lord Jesus Christ."[16] He then regularly continues with a prayer addressed to God,[17] sometimes

16. Rom. 1:7; 1 Cor. 1:3; 2 Cor. 1:2; Gal. 1:3; Eph. 1:2; Phil. 1:2; 2 Thess. 1:2; Philem. 3; cf. 1 Tim. 1:2; 2 Tim. 1:2; Titus 1:4.

17. Rom. 1:8; 1 Cor. 1:4; Phil. 1:3; 1 Thess. 1:2; 2 Thess. 1:3; Philem. 4.

also described as "the Father of our Lord Jesus Christ."[18] We could say that the reason Paul does not call God "Lord" is that he reserves the term for Jesus.

So what is going on when Jesus is called "Lord"? We need to be aware that the Greek word *kyrios* has a wide range of meaning. Basically, it denotes a social superior. It can be no more than a polite mode of address, meaning "Sir," as it is sometimes used in the Gospels when people address Jesus as *kyrios*. It can refer to an owner or an employer or the master of a slave. This is quite a common usage in the New Testament with reference to Jesus: Christians are slaves or servants of Jesus their Lord or Master. The word can refer to a ruler and therefore to God as sovereign Lord of all things. But, as we have seen, *kyrios* was also used as a regular substitute for the Divine Name, in which case it has both the connotation of rule and also the distinctive function of representing God's personal Name. This wide range of meaning sometimes makes it difficult to be sure when the word as applied to Jesus functions to refer to the Divine Name, but we can be sure that it does in a relatively large number of cases. There are, for example, a considerable number of cases of Old Testament quotations in Paul and elsewhere in the New Testament in which "the Lord" (*kyrios*) of the biblical text, representing the Divine Name, is understood to refer to Jesus. There are also standard phrases adopted from the Hebrew Bible—such as "the word of the Lord," "the day of the Lord," and (very significantly) "to call on the name of the Lord"[19]—where, in the New Testament's use, the Lord is understood to be Jesus.

If we wish to understand how early Christian writers were able to apply such texts to Jesus, a key passage is the christo-

18. 2 Cor. 1:3; Eph. 1:3; Col. 1:3.
19. Acts 9:14; 22:16; 1 Cor. 1:2; 2 Tim. 2:22.

logical hymn (as it is often called) in Philippians 2:6–11. The final part of the hymn reads:

> [9]Therefore God also highly exalted him
> and gave him the name
> that is above every name,
> [10]so that at the name of Jesus
> every knee should bend,
> in heaven and on earth and under the earth,
> [11]and every tongue should confess
> that Jesus Christ is Lord,
> to the glory of God the Father.

This should be read in relationship to a passage in the prophets, to which it unmistakably alludes:

> [18]For thus says the LORD,
> who created the heavens
> (he is God!),
> who formed the earth and made it
> (he established it;
> he did not create it a chaos,
> he formed it to be inhabited!):
> I am the LORD, and there is no other.
> . . . .
> [22]Turn to me and be saved,
> all the ends of the earth!
> For I am God, and there is no other.
> [23]By myself I have sworn,
> from my mouth has gone forth
> in righteousness
> a word that shall not return:
> "To me every knee shall bow,
> every tongue shall swear." (Isa. 45:18, 22–23)

In this magnificently monotheistic prophecy, it is YHWH, the one and only God, to whom every knee shall bow and every tongue confess. In Philippians, the same language is applied to Jesus, and the key to this usage lies in the Divine Name.

There can be no doubt that when Paul refers to "the name that is above every name," he means the Tetragrammaton.[20] No Jew could suppose otherwise. Surely this passage depicts the hallowing of God's Name for which believers pray in the Lord's Prayer. The hope of the prophets, for God to sanctify his Name in all the world, for all nations to call on the Name of the Lord, comes to fulfillment when Jesus is seen to be the revelation of God and therefore the one who shares the Divine Name with his Father.

The distribution of divine terms in Philippians 2:9–11 should be noted. On the one hand, God the Father bestows the Divine Name; on the other hand, Jesus Christ receives and bears the Name, so that he is the one confessed as Lord. Of course, this does not mean that God has given away his Name. It means that Jesus belongs to God's unique divine identity, which the Name of God names. The revelation of God in the humanity of Jesus is the way that God's identity comes to be universally known. So the confession that Jesus is the Lord redounds to the glory of God the Father. His Name is hallowed.[21]

Conclusion

The revelation of the Divine Name to Moses was the beginning of a long story of the revelation of the Name that is yet to reach its end. In giving himself the Name, God made himself

20. There is a close parallel in the Qumran Community Rule: "the name that is honored above all" (1QS 6:27). Cf. also Eph. 1:21; Heb. 1:4.

21. Other passages that speak of giving the Divine Name to Jesus are John 17:12; Heb. 1:3–4.

accessible and knowable to his people Israel. This was not for Israel's sake alone but with a view to God's revelation of himself to all nations. By giving his name to Jesus, God indicates that it is in Jesus that he makes himself knowable and accessible to all people. God has a personal Name that we acknowledge whenever we call Jesus "Lord" and whenever we pray to the Father for the hallowing of his Name.

Bibliographic Notes

On the Divine Name

André LaCocque and Paul Ricoeur, *Thinking Biblically: Exegetical and Hermeneutical Studies*, trans. David Pellauer (Chicago: University of Chicago Press, 1998), 307–61.

Tryggve D. Mettinger, *In Search of God: The Meaning and Message of the Everlasting Names*, trans. Frederick H. Cryer (Philadelphia: Fortress, 1988).

Andrea D. Saner, *"Too Much to Grasp": Exodus 3:13–15 and the Reality of God*, Journal of Theological Interpretation Supplements 11 (Winona Lake, IN: Eisenbrauns, 2015).

R. Kendall Soulen, *The Divine Name(s) and the Holy Trinity*, vol. 1, *Distinguishing the Voices* (Louisville: Westminster John Knox, 2011), chaps. 8–9.

On the Non-enunciation of the Name

Sean M. McDonough, *YHWH at Patmos: Rev. 1:4 in Its Hellenistic and Early Jewish Setting*, Wissenschaftliche Untersuchungen zum Neuen Testament 2.107 (Tübingen: Mohr Siebeck, 1999), 111–16.

On Jesus's Usage

Richard Bauckham, *Jesus: A Very Short Introduction* (Oxford: Oxford University Press, 2011), 62–68.

Richard Bauckham, "Jesus's Use of 'Father' and Disuse of 'Lord,'" in *Son of God: Divine Sonship in Jewish and Christian Antiquity*, ed. Garrick V.

Allen, Kai Akagi, Paul Sloan, and Madhavi Nevader (University Park, PA: Eisenbrauns, 2019), 87–105.

Joachim Jeremias, *New Testament Theology: The Proclamation of Jesus*, trans. John Bowden (London: SCM, 1971), 9–14, 61–68.

On Jesus as "Lord"

Richard Bauckham, *Jesus and the God of Israel: God Crucified and Other Studies on the New Testament's Christology of Divine Identity* (Grand Rapids: Eerdmans, 2008), chap. 8.

David B. Capes, *The Divine Christ: Paul, the Lord Jesus, and the Scriptures of Israel* (Grand Rapids: Baker Academic, 2018).

Chris Tilling, *Paul's Divine Christology* (Grand Rapids: Eerdmans, 2015).

3

The Revelation of the Divine Character

The third key moment of revelation is, like the second, a revelation of God made to Moses and, like the second, it is recounted in the book of Exodus, but it is much less well known than the story of the burning bush. Probably many Christians are completely unfamiliar with it. This is regrettable, not only because it is one of the most important passages in the whole Bible but also because among many Christians there are serious misconceptions about the character of God in the Old Testament that proper attention to this key moment of revelation should correct. The popular notion that the God of the Hebrew Bible is characterized by vengeance and wrath, while the God of the New Testament is, by contrast, a God of love is a travesty that deserves to be vigorously refuted. It certainly cannot survive attention to the definitive account of God's character that was given to Moses at Mount Sinai in Exodus 34.

The revelation at the burning bush answered the question "Who is God?" by revealing God's Name. Along with the Name came an indication both of God's freedom and of his commitment to Israel. The phrase "I will be who I will be" asserts God's sovereign freedom. The revelation of his Name does not give anyone control over him. But, at the same time, the revelation of the Name is God's commitment to be the God of his people Israel, the God who will lead them out of Egypt and make them his chosen people. The Name creates a relationship in which Israel can call on God by name.

But the question "Who is God?" might well expect also a different sort of answer, an answer more precisely to the questions "What is God like?" "What sort of God is he?" and "How does he characteristically behave?" The moment of revelation we shall consider in this chapter answers those kinds of questions about God. It provides in fact the fullest description of God's character to be found anywhere in the Bible. It probably tells us more about God than does anything else in the Old Testament.

After the revelation at the burning bush, the book of Exodus goes on to recount the events of the exodus from Egypt. Eventually the Israelites arrive at Mount Sinai, where God makes the covenant with them. Moses goes alone up the mountain to receive the law from God, written on stone tablets by God's own finger. But then the narrative takes a truly shocking turn. (It has been compared with adultery on one's wedding night.) The Israelites persuade Aaron to make a golden calf and proclaim it their "gods" who brought them out of Egypt (Exod. 32:1–6). Only days have elapsed since they pledged themselves to be the LORD's people and already they are repudiating him—and Moses too—and worshiping other gods. Evidently they do not want a mysterious, holy, terrifying God, hidden by the clouds at the top of a mountain that they are not allowed to approach, a God who speaks in thunder and lightning. They want a god they can get hold of and control, a god actually made for them, a god they can carry around with them.

God's *initial* response is what we might expect from the fearsome, thundering God of Sinai. God says to Moses, "Now let me alone, so that my wrath may burn hot against them and I may consume them; and of you I will make a great nation" (Exod. 32:10). God proposes to destroy his people and instead to make Moses and his descendants his covenant people. There follows a remarkable conversation between Moses and God. It is a conversation in which the very existence of Israel, together with the whole of the rest of their history, hangs in the balance. Will God destroy them in his anger or will he, unexpectedly, forgive them and remain committed to them? We cannot follow this conversation in detail here, but essentially what happens is that Moses persuades God not to destroy the people, to restore the covenant relationship that they have broken almost as soon as it began, to remain their God, and to go with them on the rest of the journey to the land he has given them. So, at the start of their history with God, Israel proves capable of shocking unfaithfulness, but God shows astonishing grace and forgiveness and commitment. Israel's failure is abject but God's grace proves more than sufficient to take them beyond it. This is a pattern that will be repeated at later junctures in Israel's history.

It may be that readers, especially modern Christian readers of Exodus, take rather for granted God's willingness to forgive. We read the story with hindsight. We know of God's abundant mercy from the rest of the biblical story. But Moses did not. When he tries to persuade God not to destroy the people, he can appeal to God's promises to the patriarchs and ask God to keep his word (Exod. 32:13). But Moses cannot not say, "I know that you are merciful and forgiving." He does not know that. So when, improbably, as it must have seemed to Moses, God does relent and forgives the people and pledges still to accompany them to the promised land, Moses finds himself wanting to know more about this God who acts in such an extraordinary way. He asks to see who God is:

> 18"Show me your glory, I pray." 19And [God] said, "I will make
> all my goodness pass before you, and will proclaim before you
> the name, 'The Lord'; and I will be gracious to whom I will
> be gracious, and will show mercy on whom I will show mercy.
> 20But," he said, "you cannot see my face; for no one shall see
> me and live." 21And the Lord continued, "See, there is a place
> by me where you shall stand on the rock; 22and while my glory
> passes by I will put you in a cleft of the rock, and I will cover
> you with my hand until I have passed by; 23then I will take away
> my hand, and you shall see my back; but my face shall not be
> seen." (Exod. 33:18–23)

God's answer to Moses's request comes in three stages, just like God's answer to Moses's question about God's Name in Exodus 3. The three stages are marked by the introductions "he said," "he said," and "the Lord continued." In Exodus 3, as we noted in the previous chapter, it was only at stage three that God actually answered Moses's question and revealed his Name. In Exodus 3, the first stage of God's answer was rather off-putting, as though God were refusing Moses's request to know God's Name. But that first stage proved to be a necessary preliminary, protecting God's freedom and transcendence, so that the giving of the Name might not be misunderstood. God's responses to Moses in Exodus 33 are rather similar. It is only at the third stage that God actually promises Moses a glimpse of his divine glory—not granting Moses's request in the way Moses doubtless intended, not promising a full vision of God's glory, but at least, for this privileged servant of God, a privileged glimpse. In Exodus 3, it was the first stage of God's answer that initially looked like a flat refusal by God to grant Moses's request. In Exodus 33 it is the second stage (v. 20) that looks like a flat refusal. The first stage (v. 19) actually echoes the words of God in Exodus 3:14, creating a link between this key moment of revelation and the key moment in Exodus 3.

So much for the parallels with Exodus 3. We must now look carefully at this passage in Exodus 33 itself. Moses asks to see God's glory. In the Hebrew Bible "glory" means something like "visible splendor." It is something that can be seen. But, as it turns out, what Moses really wants to see is God's face. For the ancient Israelites, it is the face that reveals a person. The human face is amazingly expressive. You know who someone is when you look into their face. To see God's face would be to see who God is, to penetrate the mystery of the God who characteristically hides himself in a cloud. But in God's case his face is glorious; it radiates the dazzling brightness of his divine being. As the Hebrew Bible tells us a number of times, humans cannot see God and remain alive.[1] The experience would be too overwhelming, at least in this life. God's face shines on us (Num. 6:25), but we may not look into it.

Yet God does not simply refuse Moses's request. Moses is not permitted to *see* who God is, but he is privileged to *hear* who God is. God once again speaks his Name, which Moses first heard at the burning bush, and he attaches to the Name a statement that is also reminiscent of the revelation at the bush. There, before telling Moses his Name, God prepared for doing so by saying, "I will be who I will be" (Exod. 3:14). God is the one who freely determines who he will be. He is

1. Gen. 32:30; Exod. 33:20; Judg. 6:22–23; 13:22; cf. Isa. 6:5.

not the God of Israel because he, as it were, finds himself that. Rather, he freely chooses to be Israel's God and commits himself to Israel.

That was then. Now God says, "I will be gracious to whom I will be gracious, and will show mercy on whom I will show mercy" (Exod. 33:19). The grammatical construction (a quite unusual one) is the same in each case, and the point being made is similar. Merciful and gracious as he is, God remains self-determining. His mercy cannot be controlled or manipulated. If he is being extraordinarily gracious to Israel, it is in his freedom that he chooses to do so. Among other things, this means that Moses can take no credit for having persuaded God. In a sense he has persuaded God, but not because he has some kind of leverage with God. If God opts to show mercy, it is because he freely chooses to do so.[2]

Moses is promised a revelatory encounter with God, something more than hearing God's voice out of the cloud. God will make all his goodness—another way of speaking of God's splendor or glory—pass by Moses, but Moses will be able only to glimpse God's glory as it disappears from view. This is a highly anthropomorphic account. The writer has no problem speaking of God's face, God's hand, and God's back. But the anthropomorphic language evokes something very mysterious, as the presence of God must be. Like the burning bush, this theophany is utterly unique. There is nothing else like it in Scripture.

The Revelation

The encounter that God has promised takes place the next time Moses ascends the mountain:

2. Cf. Paul's use of this text in Rom. 9:15–16.

> [5]The LORD descended in the cloud and stood with him there,
> and proclaimed the name, "The LORD." [6]The LORD passed be-
> fore him, and proclaimed,
>
> "The LORD, the LORD,
> a God merciful and gracious,
> slow to anger,
> and abounding in steadfast love and faithfulness,
> [7]keeping steadfast love for the thousandth generation,
> forgiving iniquity and transgression and sin,
> yet by no means clearing the guilty,
> but visiting the iniquity of the parents
> upon the children
> and the children's children,
> to the third and the fourth generation."
>
> [8]And Moses quickly bowed his head toward the earth, and wor-
> shiped. (Exod. 34:5–8)

At the beginning of this passage, there is a remarkable emphasis on the Divine Name. It may be that the five occurrences of the Name are intended to correspond to the five qualities in the description (merciful, gracious, slow to anger, abounding in steadfast love and faithfulness). But we should notice particularly the repetition when the LORD himself proclaims his Name ("The LORD passed before him, and proclaimed, 'The LORD, the LORD'"). Such doubling of the Name of God occurs nowhere else in the Bible. God, as it were, insists that he is *this* God, the one known by this Name, and it is this God who then describes himself as merciful, gracious, slow to anger, and abounding in steadfast love and faithfulness. It is as though God were making himself known in the way we know human persons. We first learn someone's name, learning to identify them as that particular person, and then we learn what they are like.

The character description of God falls into two parts. The first lists five qualities of character (v. 6). The second describes two characteristic ways in which God behaves (v. 7). The second part is closely parallel to what the second commandment of the Decalogue says of God (Exod. 20:5–6; Deut. 5:9–10). Both parts are frequently echoed elsewhere in the Hebrew Bible (see the appendix at the end of this chapter). Allusions to the first part are often abbreviated or varied to some extent. (Each of these qualities also frequently appears alone or in conjunction with other qualities not in this list.) Parallels to the second part of the description are most often to the positive words about God's steadfast love and forgiveness (v. 7a)[3] and sometimes also to the negative words about his judgment of sinners (v. 7b).[4] The whole character description is foundational for the biblical understanding of God.

It is the first part of the description that directly describes God's character, listing five key qualities:

a God merciful
and gracious
slow to anger
and abounding in steadfast love (*ḥesed*)
and faithfulness

The five adjectives and nouns used here are all relational terms. They describe how God relates to people (in context, specifically to Israel). Moreover, they are without exception positive. They

3. 1 Kings 8:23; 2 Chron. 6:14; Neh. 1:5; 9:32; Ps. 145:8; Dan. 9:4; Joel 2:13; Jon. 4:2.

4. Exod. 20:5–6; Deut. 5:9–10; 7:9–10; Jer. 32:18; Nah. 1:3.

portray God as overwhelmingly compassionate and caring, patient and forgiving, reliable in his commitment to his people. In other words, they reveal to Moses *the foundation in God's character* for the remarkable way God has treated Israel since the episode of the golden calf. God has chosen to have mercy because he is this sort of God.

The word *ḥesed* is not easy to translate. Modern English versions seem to have settled on the term "steadfast love." A sense of the semantic range of the word can be gathered from other translations that have been popular: "loving-kindness," "mercy," "love," "kindness," "unfailing love." The term "steadfast love" probably best captures the combination of love and loyalty conveyed by the Hebrew Bible's use of *ḥesed*. The word seems to refer primarily to loyalty in a covenant or relationship. God's *ḥesed* continues his loving commitment to his covenant people even when they abuse that relationship and reject God's ways. Faithfulness therefore goes together with steadfast love. God keeps his word. He remains faithful to his people even when they are faithless. The phrase "abounding in steadfast love and faithfulness" is literally in the Hebrew "great in steadfast love and faithfulness," giving special emphasis to these two qualities. The phrase is echoed elsewhere in Scripture,[5] and only *God* is ever said to be "*great* in steadfast love." It is a specially divine quality, a quality characteristic of the God who has committed himself to his people Israel. The context in Exodus 34, where God remains "great in steadfast love and faithfulness," even in the face of Israel's flagrant rejection of him, sets an extraordinary precedent for God's future dealings with his people, one to which later leaders and prophets are able to appeal. Israel now knows that God is unbelievably loving and unbelievably steadfast in his love.

5. Pss. 86:5, 15; 103:8; 106:45; 145:8; Isa. 63:7; Lam. 3:32; Joel 2:13; Jon. 4:2.

The rest of the description picks up the term "steadfast love" and runs with it:

> keeping steadfast love for the thousandth generation,
> forgiving iniquity and transgression and sin,
> yet by no means clearing the guilty,
> but visiting the iniquity of the parents
> upon the children
> and the children's children,
> to the third and the fourth generation. (Exod. 34:7)

In beginning to grapple with this part of the description, an aspect to be noted carefully is the contrast between "for the thousandth generation" and "to the third and the fourth generation." Whatever it means for God to "visit the iniquity" of parents on their children, God's continuing steadfast love across the generations overflows and exceeds it by far. Probably what is in mind in the latter part of this verse is the way the consequences of sin can so easily involve far more people than those who commit the sin. Human society being as it is, children suffer from their parents' culpable mistakes and failings. But these effects are limited, perhaps to the generations those parents may actually live to see: their children, grandchildren, and great-grandchildren. By contrast, God's steadfast love knows no temporal limits.

What many readers find puzzling here is that, first, there is an expansive description of God's steadfast love at work, with a strong emphasis on forgiveness of every kind of wrongdoing or rebellion ("iniquity and transgression and sin"), but then this appears to be qualified, if not contradicted, by what follows: "by no means clearing the guilty, but visiting the iniquity of the parents upon the children." There is evidently a deliberate parallelism between "forgiving iniquity" and "visiting iniquity"—that is, punishing it. But how are the two related? Does God forgive the iniquity of some people but punish the iniquity of others? (This could be suggested by the parallel in Exod. 20:6, but there is no reference to forgiveness.) Or does he forgive iniquity but nevertheless impose punishment? (This may be suggested by Lam. 3:19–33.) We shall see shortly what some other parts of the Old Testament make of this, but I will make one observation about it now.

It seems that, while God is overwhelmingly forgiving and while in some fundamental sense he can be relied on to maintain his steadfast love to his people, yet he retains the right to punish. God is guarding his self-determining freedom, which was already asserted when he said, "I will be gracious to whom I will be gracious, and I will show mercy on whom I will show mercy" (Exod. 33:19). But this need not mean that God behaves *arbitrarily*. Rather, God acts for reasons we cannot always know or understand. There is more to God's ways than we can grasp. We cannot calculate his mercy and his judgment. God abounds in steadfast love and faithfulness, and so we can rely on him to act with his people's good at heart. But the ways in which he does this may be far beyond our grasp. He remains, after all, God.

Joel and Jonah

Of the many echoes of this character description of God elsewhere in the Old Testament, we shall consider just a few of them. We begin with two closely related passages from two of the minor prophets, Joel and Jonah:

> 12Yet even now, says the LORD,
> return to me with all your heart,

with fasting, with weeping, and with mourning;
[13]rend your hearts and not your clothing.
Return to the LORD, your God,
for he is gracious and merciful,
slow to anger, and abounding in steadfast love,
and relents from punishing.
[14]Who knows whether he will not turn and relent,
and leave a blessing behind him,
a grain offering and a drink offering
for the LORD, your God? (Joel 2:12–14)

[1]But this was very displeasing to Jonah, and he became angry.
[2]He prayed to the LORD and said, "O LORD! Is not this what I
said while I was still in my own country? That is why I fled to
Tarshish at the beginning; for I knew that you are a gracious
God and merciful, slow to anger, and abounding in steadfast
love, and ready to relent from punishing. [3]And now, O LORD,
please take my life from me, for it is better for me to die than
to live. (Jon. 4:1–3)

These two passages share a particular adaptation of the formulaic description of the divine character, which first of all abbreviates the first part of the character description, reducing the five adjectives to four (gracious and merciful, slow to anger, and abounding in steadfast love). This version then adds a phrase not in Exodus 34:6–7: "and relents from punishing." It means that God, having pronounced a judgment, then changes his mind and does not carry out the punishment he had threatened.

This is an addition to the description as we find it in Exodus 34:6–7, but it draws on an earlier part of Moses's conversation with the Lord. At the beginning of the conversation, when God has declared his intention of destroying the people, Moses pleads with him to change his mind:

> Turn from your fierce wrath; change your mind and do not bring disaster on your people. (Exod. 32:12b)

> And the LORD changed his mind about the disaster that he planned to bring on his people. (32:14)

The NRSV translation makes these verses sound somewhat different from the passages in Joel and Jonah (they have "relents from punishing," while Exodus has "changed his mind about the disaster"), but the Hebrew texts are actually very close.

So Joel and Jonah both make use of a particular version of God's character description, stressing his mercy and compassion, and suggesting that in his mercy and compassion he may revoke a punishment he has threatened. We must now consider these passages in their contexts. In Joel, the prophet has spoken at length about God's judgment impending on the people (2:1–11), but now in this passage he urges them to repent and envisages that if the people repent, God may change his mind and not carry out the judgment. God's known character is made a basis for calling Israel to heartfelt, genuine repentance. It is not taken for granted that God will relent. The prophet leaves it as a question: "Who knows whether he will not turn and relent?" Again we have the implication that God cannot be controlled or manipulated by human actions. God remains free, but nevertheless his self-declared character provides ground for hope. Repentance clearly plays a major part in God's decision to revoke the judgment he announced.

Before looking more closely at the passage in Jonah, it will be helpful to consider another echo of the divine character description in yet another of the minor prophets, Nahum. Nahum's prophecy is one long oracle of judgment against the

Assyrians and their great capital city, Nineveh. It begins with this appropriate description of God:

> A jealous and avenging God is the LORD,
> the LORD is avenging and wrathful;
> the LORD takes vengeance on his adversaries
> and rages against his enemies.
> The LORD is *slow to anger* but great in power,
> and the LORD *will by no means clear the guilty.*
> (1:2–3a)

The italicized words in the last two lines echo the character description of God in Exodus 34:6–7. Unusually, the echo draws on both parts of that character description (v. 6 and v. 7). "Slow to anger" comes from the first part of the description, where it bears a positive significance, indicating God's patience with those who offend him. Nahum has selected just this one of the five qualities of God's character but then moves to the negative aspect of the second part of the description: "The LORD will by no means clear the guilty." The point is that up to now the LORD has been patient with Nineveh. He does not act impetuously, but nevertheless Nineveh's punishment is assured. Instead of the other four character traits in Exodus 34:6, the operative ones here are "jealous and avenging." Among all the echoes of Exodus 34:6 in the Hebrew Bible, this one is unique in its wholly negative thrust—that is, in making the divine character the basis for expecting judgment on God's enemies.

It is also unusual in applying the character description of God, not to his relationship with his covenant people, Israel, but to another nation, Israel's enemy. This is unusual but not unique. Jonah does the same and with the same foreign nation in view.

De Agostini Picture Library / Bridgeman Images

Figure 3. Big Fish Regurgitating Jonah. Ethiopia

The book of Jonah tells how Jonah was ordered by God actually to go to Nineveh and to prophesy God's imminent judgment on the city. Jonah does not want to do so and sets off to get as far from Nineveh as he possibly can. But he cannot escape his vocation. By means of a storm at sea and a very big fish, God ensures that Jonah goes to Nineveh, where he spends three days telling the Ninevites that the city will be overthrown in forty days' time. The Ninevites are convicted by this message. They repent and God changes his mind and revokes his judgment.

Jonah is not at all pleased. His problem all along has been that he wanted God to destroy Nineveh. He really did not want the Ninevites to hear about their coming judgment, in case they might then repent and escape God's judgment. He knew this might happen because, as he explains to God, "I knew that you are a gracious God and merciful, slow to anger, and abounding in steadfast love, and ready to relent from punishing" (Jon. 4:2). God has to teach Jonah compassion.

There are two remarkable features of the way the character description of God is deployed here. First, it is applied to God's relationship with a non-Jewish nation (as in Nahum). Second, it is applied positively (as it is not in Nahum). God deals with a foreign nation, even a great enemy of Israel, as Nineveh was, in just the same way as he deals with his covenant people. This is especially remarkable in the case of the term "steadfast love," which generally focused on God's loyal love to his covenant people. In Jonah we see the character description of God, which originally referred strictly to God's dealings with Israel, breaking out of those limits. His steadfast love no longer refers only to his covenant loyalty to his own people but also to God's consistent concern for the good of other people too. It characterizes not only who God is for Israel but simply who God is.

Psalm 145

We find the same kind of use of this character description in another remarkable text: Psalm 145:8–9.

> The Lord is gracious and merciful [*raḥûm*],
> slow to anger and abounding in steadfast love.
> The Lord is good to all,
> and his compassion [*raḥămāyw*] is over all that he
> has made.

The Hebrew words given in brackets show that "merciful" in verse 8 and "compassion" in verse 9 derive from the same Hebrew root. In these two verses the psalmist first quotes, in verse 8, the traditional character description of God, stopping short at "steadfast love" (just as Joel and Jonah do). Then he offers his own interpretation of this character description in verse 9. He explicitly universalizes it. He extends its reference beyond Israel to all people and, indeed, to all creatures: "The LORD is good to all, and his compassion is over all that he has made." The repetition of the word "all" in verse 9 is significant because it is a word that recurs no less than nineteen times in the psalm.[6] It is a psalm about the universal goodness of the God who created and rules all things. Following a single instance of "all" in verse 2 (English: "every day"), the lavish use of the word "all" in the psalm begins in earnest in verse 9, after which it occurs at least once and often twice in almost every couplet. So the psalmist is doing something very deliberate when he cites the traditional character description of God (v. 8), which in itself does not specify *to whom* God is gracious and merciful, and adds a paraphrase (v. 9) that specifies all creation as the object of his care and concern. That the psalmist really does mean all creatures, not just humans, is clear from verses 15–16, which evoke the theme, also found elsewhere in the psalms, of God's provision of food for all living creatures.[7]

However, the psalmist has not finished with the divine character description. He takes it up again in verse 13b:

> 13b The LORD is faithful in all his words,
> and gracious in all his deeds.
> 14 The LORD upholds all who are falling,
> and raises up all who are bowed down. (vv. 13b–14)

In the first line of verse 13b the psalmist picks up the fifth of the five divine qualities from Exodus 34:6, which was omitted in verse 8. Then in the second line he repeats the first of the

6. This figure refers to the Hebrew text. English translations do not quite correspond to the Hebrew in this respect.

7. Ps. 104:21, 27–28; cf. Matt. 6:26.

five ("gracious"), which already occurred first in verse 8. Here the scope of the exercise of these qualities is again universal, but initially it is expressed in the claim that God is faithful in *all* his words and gracious in *all* his deeds. God never behaves other than with faithfulness and grace—and, by implication, with mercy, patience, and steadfast love too. Then, in verse 14, the psalmist stresses that God's active faithfulness and grace includes among its recipients all the vulnerable and the afflicted. Following verses illustrate God's goodness to all his creatures in a number of other ways.

Between the two echoes of the character description of God (vv. 8–9, 13b) the psalmist has sandwiched a celebration of God's kingdom—his universal and eternal rule over all creatures (vv. 10–13a). The kingdom in these verses has the qualities we would expect of a powerful empire: glory, power, splendor, mighty deeds. But to further explicate how God rules, the psalmist has recourse to the description of the divine character from Exodus 34:6, surrounding the celebration of the kingdom with this evocation of God's grace, mercy, patience, steadfast love, and faithfulness. These are the key characteristics of God's will. In addition to the importance of this message within the psalm itself, this understanding of God's kingdom is part of the biblical background to Jesus's proclamation of the kingdom of God.

After this consistent emphasis, through most of the psalm, on God's goodness to all his creatures, verse 20 may, at least to the modern ear, seem rather a jarring conclusion:

> The Lord watches over all who love him,
> but all the wicked he will destroy.

Here the psalmist has moved on from the character description of God in Exodus 34:6 to the summary of God's characteristic behavior in 34:7: "keeping steadfast love for the thousandth generation . . . yet by no means clearing the guilty."[8] God's goodness does not mean that he will indefinitely tolerate evil. Those who will not repent of their evil must in the end perish with it. For God to be truly and finally good to his whole creation he must remove from it whatever spoils and destroys its goodness—ideally by repentance, but if necessary by judgment. Nahum and Jonah also knew this. But it is important that this element of judgment comes only after the overwhelming affirmation of God's goodness to all creatures in the rest of the psalm. Only when we have focused as intently as this psalm does on the positive qualities of God's character and the universality of his desire for the good of all his creatures can we get into proper perspective the way God deals with evil.

Conclusion—Old Testament

We have seen how, within the Old Testament, the revelation of the character of God given to Moses on Mount Sinai is taken as normative but is also interpreted and developed. Further insights into its meaning are gained as the prophets and the psalmists reflect on it. Most importantly, whereas in Exodus 34 only God's relationship with his covenant people is in view, in other texts the context broadens to all the nations and even all creation. We recall that the key terms in the description of God are relational: they refer to how God deals with people. What becomes clear in the passages we have considered in the prophets and the psalms is that these descriptions are normative for God's dealings not only with the covenant people, to whom he promised his loyalty, his special care, and his mercy,

8. See also Exod. 20:6: "showing steadfast love to the thousandth generation *of those who love me* and keep my commandments."

but also with all the other nations, who are not, or not yet, his peoples. Nevertheless, God's character is consistent. The Old Testament writers, for all their focus on God's chosen people, see that if this is how God is, it must be how he is in his dealings with all people and all creation.

God's Character Seen in Jesus

So important is this character description of God in the Old Testament, it would be surprising if the writers of the New Testament ignored it. In fact, there are few explicit allusions to Exodus 34:6–7 in the New Testament, but there is one place where it is brought into important relationship to the revelation of God in Jesus Christ. This is in the Prologue to the Gospel of John.

The primary function of the Prologue is to show readers of the Gospel how, starting from the Old Testament, they should understand the story of Jesus that follows in the rest of the Gospel. (Thus it begins with an echo of the very beginning of the Torah, "in the beginning," and continues with further allusions to Gen. 1.) The key passage for our present interest is at the end of the Prologue:

> [14]And the Word became flesh and lived among us, and we have seen his glory, the glory as of the Only One from the Father, full of grace and truth. . . . [16]From his fullness we have all received, grace upon grace. [17]The law indeed was given through Moses; grace and truth came through Jesus Christ. [18]No one has ever seen God. It is the Only One, himself God, who is in the bosom of the Father, who has made him known. (John 1:14, 16–18 NRSV alt.)

The references to Moses take us back to the book of Exodus. John is very positive here about the law of Moses. God's grace to his people was expressed in the Sinai covenant. So the incarnation of the Word and the revelation of God in Jesus can be called "grace upon grace" (v. 16), meaning "grace in addition to the grace already given at Sinai." The old covenant was grace and Jesus Christ is more grace. Yet the old covenant had its limitations. When we read, "No one has ever seen God," we cannot but recall that Moses was not allowed to see God's face (Exod. 33:23). When John says that no one has ever seen God, he is not denying the visions of God that were granted to a number of privileged individuals in the Old Testament.[9] He means that they did not see God's face. As we noticed in discussing Exodus 33, it is in the face that one really sees who someone is. So the implication of John's statement is that no one has ever seen who God is. Glimpses of glory, like that granted to Moses, there have been, but not the insight into what God is like that only his face could give. Moses, we recall, heard what God is like but could not see it. Even in that remarkable moment of encounter with God, God remained hidden, covering Moses's eyes to keep him from seeing (Exod. 33:22).

Moses's inability to see God contrasts with the words of John 1:14: "The Word became flesh and we have seen his glory." The "we" in this verse are the eyewitnesses, the disciples of Jesus who actually saw Jesus in his physical visibility and were granted the spiritual insight to see the divine glory in that physical person and life of Jesus. (So the "we" of v. 14 are not the same as "we all" in v. 16. The latter are all Christian believers.) Because Jesus is the only Son of his Father, the glory these eyewitnesses saw as "his" was the reflected glory of his Father. It was "glory as of the Only One from the Father, full of grace and truth."

9. E.g., Exod. 24:9–11; 1 Kings 22:19–22; Isa. 6:1–4; Ezek. 1:4–28; 10:1–22; Dan. 7:9–10.

We might not immediately recognize the allusion to Exodus 34:6. These are the words that correspond:

> abounding in steadfast love and faithfulness (*rab-ḥesed we-ʾĕmet*)

> full of grace and truth (*plērēs charitos kai alētheias*)

As in many of the Old Testament's allusions to the divine character description, John has summed up the five qualities by selecting two of them. But he has imitated the structure of the last part of the description—"abounding in steadfast love and faithfulness"—in his phrase "full of grace and truth." The Hebrew word for "faithfulness" (*emet*) is often translated in the Greek Bible as *alētheia*, "truth." Faithfulness is being true to one's word. Faithfulness is truth as a personal characteristic. For *ḥesed*, "steadfast love," John seems to use the Greek word *charis*, "grace," which is an unusual translation, though certainly not impossible.[10] John may have chosen it not simply to translate *ḥesed* but to summarize all four of the first four qualities: merciful, gracious, slow to anger, steadfast love. All four of these amount to God's generosity to his people, which is the meaning of "grace." John is saying that Jesus manifested in his person and life the character of God—full of grace and truth. What Moses had heard but had not been allowed to see, Jesus made visible: "We have seen his glory" (John 1:14).

John has described the law of Moses as "grace" and the incarnation as "grace in addition to grace." But he also contrasts the law with Jesus Christ: "The law indeed was given through Moses; grace and truth came [*egeneto*] through Jesus Christ" (John 1:17). The verb *egeneto* here means something like "came

10. In the Greek Bible, *ḥesed* is usually translated as *eleos*. *Charis* is used in Esther 2:9, 17; Sir. 7:33; 40:17.

about" or "happened." The divine character—"steadfast love and faithfulness" or "grace and truth"—happened in Jesus. Jesus's whole being and story were the steadfast love and faithfulness of God in action.

Therefore, "It is the Only One, himself God, who is in the bosom of the Father, who has made him known" (John 1:18b). No human, not even Moses, has seen who God is in the holy splendor of his face. But the Only One, because he is uniquely close to the Father, because he gazes into that face that expresses the infinite goodness of God, alone has made him known. We could translate the last phrase as "has described him [*exēgēsato*]."

In the third century BC, the great Jewish sage Ben Sira summoned his readers to glorify the Lord with all their powers, because they could never match his inexpressible greatness:

> 30Glorify the Lord and exalt him as much as you can,
> for he surpasses even that.
> When you exalt him, summon all your strength,
> and do not grow weary, for you cannot praise him enough.
> 31Who has seen him and can describe him?
> Or who can extol him as he is? (Sir. 43:30–31)

Ben Sira's question "Who has seen him and can describe him?" is, of course, a rhetorical question, but John, in effect, answers it. Only the utterly Unique One has seen him and so can describe him. That description is the life, death, and resurrection of Jesus. More than once, this Gospel says that whoever has seen Jesus has seen the Father (John 12:45; 14:9). The extraordinary message of the Gospel is that only human flesh in its visibility could make that true.

So the character of God, which Moses heard God describe in words, is described visibly in the flesh of Jesus, the character of his life and his death, "full of grace and truth." In the rest of John's Gospel, "truth" is a divine attribute often ascribed to Jesus. For example, he is "the way, and the truth, and the life" (14:6). But the word grace (*charis*) is never used in the Gospel after the Prologue. In the space of three verses of the Prologue, John uses the word four times ("grace and truth," "grace upon grace," "grace and truth") but never uses it again. If "grace" in the Prologue sums up those first four qualities in the divine description (merciful, gracious, slow to anger, steadfast love) and if that verbal description was made visible in Jesus, it seems strange that John then drops the word "grace" and never uses it again in the rest of the Gospel.

The reason must be that the word "love" (*agapē*) takes over as John's summary of what God is like. He uses the cognate verb (*agapaō*) for the first time in the well-known summary of the Gospel's story: "God so loved the world that he gave his only Son, so that everyone who believes in him may not perish but may have everlasting life" (3:16 NRSV alt.). This means that the merciful, generous, gracious character of God is seen in action in the events of the Gospel. John does not use the noun "love" (*agapē*) very often (seven times), but he uses the verb "to love" (*agapaō*) frequently (thirty-seven times). His Gospel is about God's love *happening*. The word *charis* ("grace") would not have supplied him with a corresponding verb to describe all that *happening* of grace and truth, the divine love occurring in the story of Jesus.[11]

There is another good reason why John, as it were, translated "grace" in the Prologue into "love" in the rest of the Gospel. The incarnation not only revealed God's character in visible

11. The word *charizomai*, which is occasionally used in the New Testament, means either "to grant" *something* (which needs to be specified) or "to forgive." Thus while *charis* is frequent in the Pauline literature, *charizomai* is rare.

form, in the concrete person and life and death of the man Jesus. It also revealed the loving relationship between the Father and the Son, the love of the Father for the only Son who is in his bosom, and the Son's love for his Father.[12] In other words, the incarnation reveals not only, as in Exodus 34, what God is like in his relationship with the world but also what God is like in his inner being. The eternal love between the Father and the Son is the source from which the love of God overflows into the world in the incarnation of the Son and his death for the life of the world. God is love in himself as well as in relation to his creation, and he is love in relation to his creation because he is eternally love in himself.

Bibliographic Notes

On Exodus 34:6–7 and Related Texts

Mark J. Boda, *The Heartbeat of Old Testament Theology: Three Creedal Expressions* (Grand Rapids: Baker Academic, 2017), chap. 3.

Walter Brueggemann, *Theology of the Old Testament: Testimony, Dispute, Advocacy* (Minneapolis: Fortress, 1997), chap. 5.

Thomas B. Dozeman, "Inner-Biblical Interpretation of Yahweh's Gracious and Compassionate Character," *Journal of Biblical Literature* 108 (1989): 207–23.

R. Walter L. Moberly, *At the Mountain of God: Story and Theology in Exodus 32–34*, Journal for the Study of the Old Testament Supplement Series 22 (Sheffield: Sheffield Academic, 1983).

On Ḥesed (*Steadfast Love*)

A very accessible treatment is Michael Card, *Inexpressible: Hesed and the Mystery of God's Lovingkindness* (Downers Grove, IL: IVP Books, 2018).

12. John 1:18; 5:20; 10:15; 14:31; 17:24.

Gordon R. Clark, *The Word "Hesed" in the Hebrew Bible*, Journal for the Study of the Old Testament Supplement Series 157 (Sheffield: Sheffield Academic, 1993).

Katharine Sakenfeld, *The Meaning of* Hesed *in the Hebrew Bible: A New Inquiry*, Harvard Semitic Monographs 17 (Missoula, MT: Scholars Press, 1978).

On Exodus 34 and the Prologue to John's Gospel

Alexander Tsutserov, *Glory, Grace, and Truth: Ratification of the Sinaitic Covenant according to the Gospel of John* (Eugene, OR: Pickwick, 2009).

Appendix

Allusions to Exodus 34:6–7

Parallels to Exodus 34:6	Parallels to Exodus 34:7
Numbers 14:18	Exodus 20:5–6
2 Chronicles 30:9	*Numbers 14:18*
Nehemiah 9:17, 31	Deuteronomy 5:9–10
Psalm 25:6	Deuteronomy 7:9–10
Psalm 77:8–9	1 Kings 8:23
Psalm 78:38	2 Chronicles 6:14
Psalm 85:10–11	Nehemiah 1:5
Psalm 86:5, 15	Nehemiah 9:32
Psalm 103:8	Jeremiah 32:18
Psalm 106:45	Daniel 9:4
Psalm 111:4	*Nahum 1:3*
Psalm 116:5	
Psalm 145:8, 13	
Isaiah 63:7	
Lamentations 3:32	
Hosea 2:19–20	
Joel 2:13	
Jonah 4:2	
Nahum 1:3	
John 1:14	
Romans 2:4	
Ephesians 2:4	
James 5:11	

Note: Parallels to both verses of Exodus 34:6–7 are italicized. I do not suggest that the authors of all these texts were necessarily dependent on the text of Exodus 34:6–7. They may have known this character description of God in other ways.

4

The Revelation of the Trinity

In this chapter we shall focus on three key moments of revelation in the Gospel of Mark. These three moments of revelation occur at critical points in the story of Jesus as Mark tells it. The first one, close to the beginning of the story and the first episode in which Jesus himself features, is the vision that Jesus receives at the time of his baptism (1:9–11). The last of the three, consisting of the tearing of the veil of the temple and the confession of the centurion, occurs at the time of Jesus's death and is close to the end of the Gospel (15:37–39). The second of the three is the transfiguration of Jesus on the mountaintop, which occurs at what is generally regarded as the midpoint of Mark's story (9:2–8). These are not the only moments of revelation in the Gospel. For example, there is also the message the angel gives to the women at the tomb, right at the end of the Gospel (16:6–7). But the three key moments I have listed seem to be highlighted by Mark and deliberately linked as a series of events in which the core meaning of Mark's story comes to light.

It will be good to have all three passages in mind as we proceed.

The Vision at the Baptism (Mark 1:9–11 NRSV alt.)

[9]In those days Jesus came from Nazareth of Galilee and was
baptized by John in the Jordan. [10]And just as he was coming up
out of the water, he saw the heavens torn apart and the Spirit
descending like a dove on him. [11]And a voice came from heaven,
"You are my beloved Son; with you I am well pleased."

The Transfiguration (Mark 9:2–8 NRSV alt.)

[2]Six days later, Jesus took with him Peter and James and John,
and led them up a high mountain apart, by themselves. And he
was transfigured before them, [3]and his clothes became dazzling
white, such as no one on earth could bleach them. [4]And there
appeared to them Elijah with Moses, who were talking with
Jesus. [5]Then Peter said to Jesus, "Rabbi, it is good for us to be
here; let us make three dwellings, one for you, one for Moses,
and one for Elijah." [6]He did not know what to say, for they
were terrified. [7]Then a cloud overshadowed them, and from
the cloud there came a voice, **"This is my beloved Son; listen
to him!"** [8]Suddenly when they looked around, they saw no one
with them any more, but only Jesus.

The Centurion's Confession (Mark 15:37–39)

[37]Then Jesus gave a loud cry and breathed his last. [38]And the curtain of the temple was torn in two, from top to bottom. [39]Now
when the centurion, who stood facing him, saw that in this way
he breathed his last, he said, **"Truly this man was God's Son!"**

Several features of these narratives tie them together (see table 4.2 at the end of the chapter). In the first two of them we hear the voice of God (the only occasions in Mark's Gospel in which

God himself speaks). In both these cases, God refers to Jesus as his "beloved Son" (a phrase used only in these two passages of the Gospel). Both are declarations that Jesus is God's Son, and the same is true of the third passage, where it is not God but the centurion at the cross who declares Jesus to be God's Son. So there is a difference in the third case, but all three are revelations of Jesus's identity as God's Son.

Those observations might suggest that, while the baptism and the transfiguration belong closely together, the third of these moments of revelation is less closely connected. But Mark also writes in such a way as to tie the first and last of the three moments of revelation closely together. In Jesus's vision at his baptism, he sees the heavens "torn apart." That is a very unusual phrase. More often in the Bible visions occur when the heavens are opened.[1] In fact, Matthew and Luke use the word "opened," rather than "torn apart," in their versions of Jesus's vision at his baptism (Matt. 3:16; Luke 3:21). But Mark has this strikingly violent image of the sky torn apart. The Greek verb he uses, *schizō*, is used only eleven times in the New Testament, and only twice by Mark, once here and again at 15:38, where he uses the same verb to describe the extraordinary event that occurred in the temple at the time of Jesus's death: the veil was torn in two. This must be a deliberate echo of 1:10, a verbal indication of a connection between the two events.

There is another verbal link between the first and last moments of revelation in the word *pneuma*, "spirit." At the baptism, Jesus sees the Spirit come down onto him, and then God calls him his "beloved Son." The moment of Jesus's death Mark describes by means of a verb related to the word *pneuma*. In 15:39, he says that Jesus expired (*exepneusen*, from the verb *ekpneō*). (The English words "spirit" and "expired" are similarly

1. Ezek. 1:1; John 1:51; Acts 7:56; 10:11; Rev. 19:11.

related.) The NRSV translates the verb in 15:39 as "he breathed his last." A basic meaning of *pneuma* is "breath," and so the verb *ekpneō* means "to breathe out." Jesus breathed out, he breathed his last, the breath of life left him, and the centurion, seeing (as Mark emphasizes) that Jesus expired, declared him to be God's Son (15:39). Like *schizō*, the verb *ekpneō* is quite unusual. Mark uses it only here and it occurs only once elsewhere in the New Testament, when Luke also uses it with reference to Jesus's death (23:46). It seems very likely that by means of the words *pneuma* and *exepneusen*, Mark has made a deliberate verbal link between Jesus's baptismal vision and his death.

These three moments of revelation are presented by Mark as a series that structures his whole story. The first and the last of them enclose most of the story, while the second occurs significantly at the midpoint (see table 4.1 at the end of the chapter).

The Baptismal Vision

Mark's story of Jesus's baptism and vision features not only Jesus's first appearance in the Gospel. It is also an "appearance" of all three persons of the Trinity. By putting it like that I am using later theological language that Mark would not have recognized, but I think this language expresses a legitimate reading of the story. This is a Trinitarian event. It is not a static representation of the Trinity in eternity or in heaven. Rather, it is the beginning of the Trinitarian story that Mark's Gospel tells. Up until this point in the biblical story, God had not been perceived as Trinity because God did not, in the Old Testament story, act in a way that revealed God as Trinity. Christians have often found hints of the Trinity in the Old Testament, but they could not have been seen at the time. What brought the early Christians to understand God as Trinity was the story of Jesus, the story that Mark and other Gospels tell, because here God made himself known through Jesus. The eternal relationship of the Father and the Son within the Trinity now took earthly form in the human Jesus and his relationship with his Father, while the Spirit of God became known as the Spirit that empowered Jesus and the Spirit Jesus himself gave to his disciples.

So here at the outset of Jesus's ministry the three divine actors in the story make their appearance. The story takes place on earth, but it is initiated from heaven. Jesus sees the heavens torn apart. He does not, like some biblical visionaries, see into heaven. He does not see the throne of God in heaven. What he sees is the Spirit of God coming down out of heaven in the form of a dove. There are two questions to ask about the way Mark describes the vision. First, why, in 1:10, does he use the word "torn apart" or "ripped apart" (*schizomenous*) when the way one would expect such a vision to be described would be that Jesus saw the heavens "opened"? The prophet Ezekiel's visions occurred when he saw heaven opened (Ezek. 1:1); Stephen's vision of Jesus at the right hand of God took place when heaven opened and he was able to see into heaven (Acts 7:56); Peter, in a dream, saw heaven opened and a package being lowered to earth (Acts 10:11); and, in the book of Revelation, the prophet John saw a door opened in heaven so that he could ascend into heaven (Rev. 4:1). So why does Mark depart from the usual terminology? The answer lies in a passage of prophecy: Isaiah 63:15–64:1.

In his prologue, Mark has already signaled that his story is a fulfillment of the prophecies of Isaiah.[2] The later chapters of Isaiah (from chap. 40 onward) were probably for the early Christians the most important part of the Bible. In this passage the prophet has been speaking on behalf of the faithful within

2. Mark 1:2–3, a quotation that combines Isa. 40:3 and Mal. 3:1.

Israel at a time when it seemed as though God had abandoned them. He has been recalling the way God had saved Israel from Egypt in the dramatic events of the exodus from Egypt, and he begs God to do something like that again:

> [15]Look down from heaven and see,
> from your holy and glorious habitation.
> Where are your zeal and your might?
> The yearning of your heart and your compassion?
> They are withheld from me.
> [16]For you are our father,
> though Abraham does not know us
> and Israel [i.e., Jacob] does not acknowledge us;
> you, O LORD, are our father;
> our Redeemer from of old is your name.
> [17a]Why, O LORD, do you make us stray from your ways
> and harden our heart, so that we do not fear you?
> . . . .
> [19]We have long been like those whom you do not rule,
> like those not called by your name. (Isa. 63:15–17a, 19)

> [1]O that you would tear open the heavens and come down,
> so that the mountains would quake at your presence. (64:1)

In the days of Moses, God came down to Mount Sinai and the mountains quaked (Ps. 68:7–8; Hab. 3:6, 10). The prophet is saying to God: we need you to do something like that again. He wants God to come down in power to redeem his people again. The image of tearing the heavens apart is appropriate here because it suggests that irruption of divine power into the world.

So when Mark uses the same image, it means that the prophet's prayer is at last being answered. No longer are the people to be bereft of the powerful divine presence with them. True, the mountains are not quaking. The form of this *new* exodus that Mark is narrating is not entirely what was expected, and so far only Jesus knows what is happening. But God has come down from heaven. As the human Jesus, God's Son, empowered for ministry by the divine Spirit sent from heaven, God is powerfully present among his people once again.

The second question we must ask about what Jesus sees in the vision concerns the dove. Jesus sees the Spirit descend on him like a dove. Does that mean that the Spirit is like a dove or that the Spirit descends in the manner of a dove? Commentators disagree, but most probably Mark means that Jesus sees the Spirit in the form of a dove. Otherwise, how does he see the Spirit at all?

For the Spirit in this context to be represented as a bird is easily understandable. A bird could cover the distance from heaven to earth and then perch on Jesus's head. But why a dove? Nowhere else in the Bible or in Second Temple Jewish literature is the dove a symbol of the Spirit. There is just one passage in rabbinic literature—in the Babylonian Talmud—in which the Spirit is compared with a dove. Shimon ben Zoma, who was well known as an exegete of the first chapter of Genesis, is said to have referred to the text "The Spirit of God hovered over the face of the waters" (Gen. 1:2b)[3] and to have commented, "Like a dove that hovers over her young without actually touching them" (b. Ḥag. 15a). The comment is reported to have been made at a time when the temple was still standing (i.e., before AD 70), but whether it was really uttered by Ben Zoma at that date is far from sure. If the dove at Jesus's baptism could be

3. This is the translation presupposed by Ben Zoma's comment.

associated with the Spirit as depicted in Genesis 1:2b, then the meaning could be that the Spirit descending onto Jesus was initiating the work of new creation, the renewal of all creation by the same divine Spirit that was active in the original creation. But there is nothing else in the story that alludes to the theme of new creation.

It is possible that the particular species of bird has no significance. (The dove is a common species in Palestine.) But I have a speculative, new suggestion of my own to make, which came to me while I was preparing the content of this chapter. The Hebrew word for dove is *yônāh*. The word is familiar to readers of the Bible in English in the form of the name Jonah, which means "dove." It comprises four Hebrew letters (יונה: *yōd*, *wāw*, *nûn*, *hē*), like the Divine Name, the Tetragrammaton (יהוה: *yōd*, *hē*, *wāw*, *hē*). Three of its letters are the same as three of the letters of the Divine Name. It looks quite like the Divine Name. In chapter 2 we noticed that in the story of the burning bush, there is a play on words between the Hebrew word *ʾehyeh* (meaning "I am" or "I will be") and the Divine Name (YHWH). The word *ʾehyeh* is a case of a four-letter word (*aleph*, *hē*, *yōd*, *hē*) that has three of its letters in common with the Divine Name. So my suggestion is that, in a period when Jews no longer spoke the Divine Name but still wrote it, it would be easy to see an association between the Divine Name and the Hebrew word for "dove." What better symbol for the Spirit of the LORD than a bird whose name resembles the name of the LORD?

We can now consider the words of the voice from heaven. God calls Jesus his beloved Son. He does not say merely, "You are my son," which is how God addresses the Messiah in Psalm 2:7, but "You are my beloved Son." Moreover, the word "beloved" (*agapētos*), when used of a son or daughter, often has the sense of "the only child," the child who is especially loved because he or she is the only child. For example, when, in the story of Abraham's sacrifice of his son Isaac, the Hebrew text calls Isaac Abraham's only son (Gen. 22:2, 12, 16), this is translated in the Greek version of the Old Testament by *agapētos*, "beloved." In the Hebrew, God says to Abraham, "Take your son, your only son Isaac, whom you love" (Gen. 22:2). In the Greek this becomes, "Take your beloved son Isaac, whom you love." Something similar happens in the story of Jephthah's daughter, another case of a father being obliged to sacrifice a beloved child. The Hebrew says simply that she was Jephthah's only child (Judg. 11:34), but the Greek version says that she was his "beloved only child" (using the word *agapētos*). The translator wanted to convey the two aspects of the Hebrew word—indicating both an only child and a beloved child. So we can say that the heavenly voice in Mark's story declares Jesus to be God's only and beloved Son. If other humans or angels might be called sons of God for various reasons,[4] Jesus is singled out as son in a unique sense, his Father's only son, and moreover dear to his Father's heart. For him to be God's son is no mere status or office. The phrase is an affective one, expressing emotional attachment and commitment.[5]

Many scholars claim that the title "Son of God" in Mark is a messianic title that means no more than that Jesus is a human being appointed by God to act as God's agent in bringing salvation. It is true that, according to a very small number of texts in the Old Testament, the king could be called God's son,[6] and it is true that, in an equally small number of texts from the Jewish literature of the New Testament period, the royal Messiah, the

4. E.g., Gen. 6:2; Job 1:6; Ps. 82:6.

5. That the language is affective can be seen in Gen. 22:12, 16; Jer. 31:20.

6. 2 Sam. 7:14; 1 Chron. 17:13; Pss. 2:7; 89:26. But in the late Second Temple period, these texts were understood to refer not to the kings of the biblical period but to the ideal king, the Messiah, of the future.

expected son of David, is called "Son of God."[7] But such texts are remarkably rare. They do not explain why Mark and other New Testament writers give such prominence to the term "Son of God" applied to Jesus. For Mark, as for other New Testament authors, it is the most meaningful description of Jesus. As we can see in the words of God in Jesus's baptismal vision, Jesus is God's beloved Son. The term refers not merely to a status or office to which Jesus is appointed but to a profound relationship that binds Father and Son together.

Out of this relationship there does, certainly, arise a role and a task, for which God is at this point equipping his Son. For the heavenly voice continues with "in whom I have been well pleased." This is a clear allusion to another part of the prophecies of Isaiah:

> Here is my servant, whom I uphold,
> my chosen, in whom my soul delights;
> I have put my spirit upon him;
> he will bring forth justice to the nations. (42:1)

This is the servant of the LORD, anointed with God's Spirit, whom God has appointed for a unique role in his history with the world (see also Isa. 61:1). The Spirit is God's enabling presence with Jesus, equipping him for his messianic task. At the same time, the biblical phrase that expresses God's choice of Jesus for this role—"in whom my soul delights"—also continues the note of close relationship that "my beloved Son" evokes.

From this point on in his Gospel, Mark's spotlight is on Jesus, rather than on the Spirit or the Father, but the baptismal vision has set the stage for us readers so that we know that the

7. 4Q174 1–3:1:11; 4Q246 2:1(?); 4 Ezra 7:28; 13:32, 37, 52(?). Only the first of these (a quotation of 2 Sam. 7:14) is likely to be an instance of "Son of God" applied to the Messiah.

Spirit is continuously at work in Jesus's ministry (cf. Mark 3:29) and that Jesus is continuously in touch with his heavenly Father, sustained by his Father's love and carrying out his Father's will to the end. Of this relationship with his Father, readers of Mark are reminded especially by Jesus's prayer in Gethsemane (14:36), as well as by the two other key moments of revelation, to which we now turn.

The Transfiguration

Before discussing this second moment of revelation, we need to recall some of what has happened in Mark's story of Jesus's ministry up to this point. Jesus has healed the sick and cast out demons; he has forgiven sins; he has stilled a storm and walked on the water; he has miraculously fed large crowds of people. It is on the basis of all this evidence that, when Jesus asks his disciples who they think he is, Peter, speaking for them all, is able to say, "You are the Messiah" (8:29). Peter means, "You are the expected king of Israel, the new David." But immediately Jesus begins to explain to the disciples that he is going to suffer and to be rejected by the Jewish authorities and to be put to death before rising from the dead. Peter is scandalized. This is not at all what he thinks should happen to the Messiah.

Then, six days later, Jesus takes three of the disciples with him up a high mountain, where they are given an extraordinary experience, a moment of divine disclosure. First, they see Jesus "transfigured," meaning that his appearance is radically changed. This is a foretaste of Jesus's divine glory. They see him as he will appear at his coming in glory in the future. Whereas Matthew and Luke refer to his face (Matt. 17:2; Luke 9:29), Mark focuses on his clothes, because it enables him to say that they became “dazzling white, such as no one on earth could bleach them” (9:3). Heavenly beings in the Bible and the Jewish tradition are usually shining, radiating light like the sun or the stars, and their clothes, too, are dazzling, unearthly in their splendor (Dan. 7:9; Rev. 4:4).

Jesus is joined by two eminent figures from Israel’s history, great prophets of the past. Scholars have debated the significance of this. Why Moses and Elijah? In my view, the main point is that Jesus turns out to be not in the same category as Moses and Elijah but decisively distinguished from them. Peter makes the mistake of thinking all three are, as it were, on the same level. For Jesus to be as great and glorious as Moses and Elijah would, after all, be stupendous enough. So Peter suggests making three temporary dwellings, one for each of the three. What he may have been thinking is that these must be the three great figures of the messianic age. The Jewish hope was for the restoration of the nation of Israel to their properly constituted theocratic state. This required three anointed leaders: a king of the line of David, a high priest descended from Aaron, and a prophet. Peter already knows that Jesus is the anointed king, the Messiah. One Jewish view at the time was that Elijah would return as the high priest of the renewed Israel.[8] (In other forms of Jewish expectation, Elijah was to come as the prophet of the last days.) If Jesus were the king and Elijah the high priest, then Moses, the greatest of the prophets, would be the prophet in this ideally reconstituted Israel. So Peter makes his inept suggestion of honoring each of them with some sort of tent. Maybe he thinks the messianic kingdom is going to be inaugurated, then and there, on the mountain.

If these were Peter’s thoughts, they are sharply contradicted by the divine voice. Ignoring Moses and Elijah, God specifies

8. Pseudo-Philo, *Biblical Antiquities* 48:1.

Jesus as his beloved Son: "*This* is my beloved Son" (Mark 9:7 NRSV alt.). What the heavenly voice had said to Jesus at his baptism, God now reveals to the three disciples. In doing so, the voice singles Jesus out as unique. He is not one of a triumvirate of equals, not even along with Moses and Elijah. Even Peter's recognition of Jesus as Messiah evidently did not go far enough. Jesus is God's unique and uniquely beloved Son. When the three disciples look around, they see that Moses and Elijah have gone, taken up in the overshadowing cloud, but Jesus is still there with them. He is the one to whom they should listen.

When we recall what happened just before the transfiguration—Peter's confession of Jesus as Messiah, followed by Jesus's prediction of his future suffering and death, and Peter's well-meaning, scandalized reaction—then there is something else to be said about Moses and Elijah. Both faced bitter opposition. Their ministries were attended by rejection and suffering. Thus far they foreshadowed what was to come for Jesus. But for neither Moses nor Elijah did the opposition lead to violent death. Moses died peacefully and honored at an advanced age. Elijah was taken up to heaven in a whirlwind. But for Jesus the bitter opposition he is to encounter will lead to his being put to death, as he has just recently tried to get across to Peter and the others. Paradoxically, being the beloved Son puts him in a special category that entails his violent death. God did not let Moses or Elijah suffer such a fate, but his unique and dearly beloved Son—him God will hand over to mocking, torture, and an abandoned death.

Jesus had explained this to Peter, but Peter would not listen. So now the divine command comes: "This is my beloved Son; *listen to him*!" (Mark 9:7). This is why the command comes at this midpoint in Mark's story, when Jesus has begun to teach the disciples about his coming passion and death. It is what they do not want to hear and do not want to understand. So they are told to listen, as Jesus will continue to teach them what

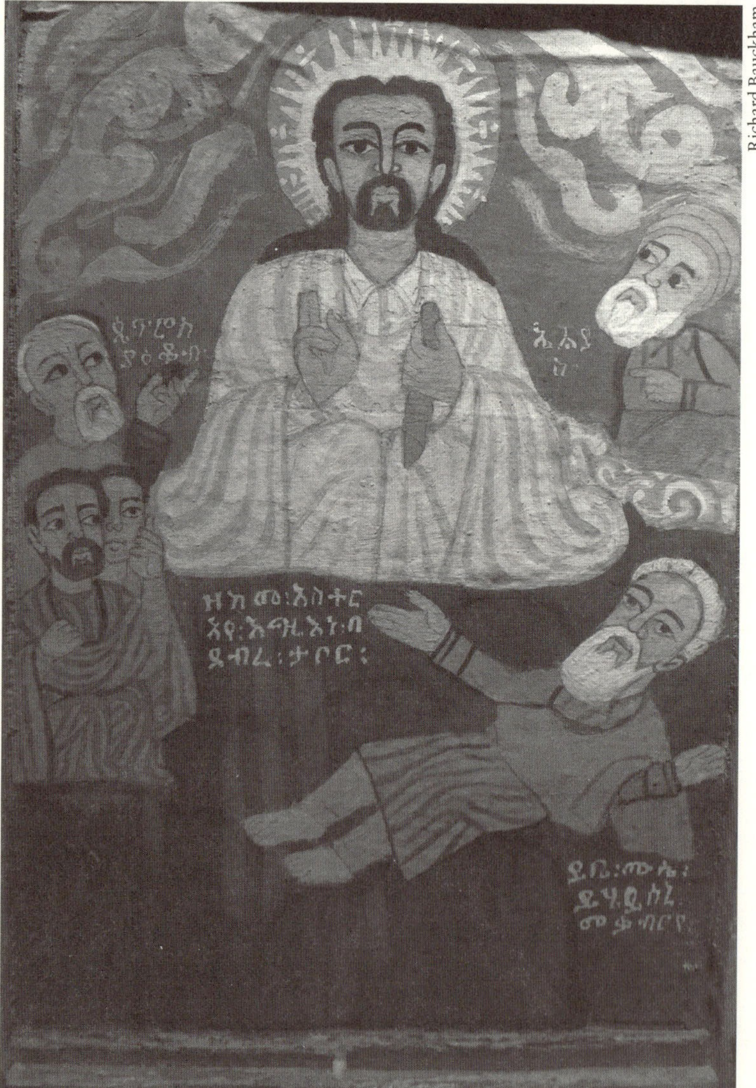

Richard Bauckham

Figure 4. Transfiguration. Institute of Ethiopian Studies, Addis Ababa, Ethiopia

being the beloved Son is going to require of him. Certainly they will see him again in heavenly glory, but not yet. The transfiguration was only a foretaste, a memorable, reassuring, empowering foretaste of the ultimate future beyond the cross. First, the disciples must follow Jesus on his way to the cross.

The Centurion's Confession

The third moment of revelation is the moment of Jesus's death. Two quite different things happen that only for us readers compose a single revelatory moment. The centurion did not see the temple veil torn in two. Maybe no one at all saw it, or, if anyone did, just a few priests. The centurion did not speak his remarkable insight for anyone at that time and place to hear, but it is a revelation to us. This is the third time Jesus is declared God's Son, but this time not by God but by a human being who sees Jesus die.

We need to look again at the correspondences between the vision of Jesus at his baptism and the events that immediately follow his death (see table 4.2). We have already noticed the verbal link between the Spirit (*pneuma*) at the baptism and Mark's way of referring to Jesus's death: "he expired" (*exepneusen*). It has been suggested that Mark intends us to understand that the divine Spirit that descended on Jesus at the start of his ministry left Jesus at the moment of his death. This is not plausible. If Mark meant that, he would have expressed it more clearly. At the literal level, Mark is using an accepted term for dying, where the *pneuma* is ordinary breath. But what is likely is that Mark means this to *symbolize* the theological truth that the death of Jesus released the Spirit of God into the world. During Jesus's ministry, the Spirit was active only in Jesus's presence and activity. After Jesus's death, the Spirit becomes the Spirit of Jesus Christ at work in his name in the world. The point is not that the Spirit left Jesus but that the Spirit went forth from Jesus to continue his work, beyond the bounds of his physical presence, throughout the world.

If that is the case, it may help us to understand the significance of the next thing that happens in Mark's narrative of Jesus's death: "The curtain of the temple was torn in two, from top to bottom" (15:38). A wide range of suggestions have been made as to the significance of this event. We can at least take it that Mark intends us to see a moment of revelation here. The rending of the curtain in the temple tells us something about Jesus, as the vision at his baptism does and as the transfiguration does. In each case something revelatory is *seen* (by Jesus, by the disciples, by us readers) before a voice is *heard* declaring Jesus to be God's Son. Moreover, we have already noticed the parallel use of the same verb (*schizō*) for the tearing apart of the heavens and the tearing apart of the temple veil, and we have seen that Mark's choice of this word in the context of the baptismal vision indicates the fulfillment of the prophet's prayer that God "would tear open the heavens and come down" (Isa. 64:1). I think we should probably see the ripping of the temple curtain as a second stage of that fulfillment.

There were two curtains in the temple. The outer one, at the entrance to the sanctuary building, hid the holy place from the eyes of all except the priests who entered the holy place and ministered there in God's presence, burning incense and offering the showbread. Another curtain separated the holy place from the innermost sanctuary, the holy of holies, where God himself dwelled.

No one was allowed to enter the holy of holies, except the high priest once a year on the day of atonement. It was the holiest spot on earth, and the curtain shielded the priests and the people from the dangerously holy presence of God. Almost certainly it is this curtain, the inner veil, to which Mark refers.

I suggest we may see a parallel between the heavens in the baptismal vision and the curtain of the temple. The heavens (the sky) are a sort of curtain separating God's heavenly dwelling place from the world, while the curtain of the temple separated God's earthly dwelling place from the world. At the outset of Jesus's ministry God tore apart the curtain of the heavens in order to come down and be present and active in Jesus. At Jesus's death he tore apart the curtain in the temple in order to come out and be present and active through Jesus in the world at large. If there was a sense in which God's presence on earth was confined to the temple, this is no longer true. If there was a sense in which his presence on earth in the temple made him accessible to his people Israel but not to the rest of the nations, that too is no longer true. The point is not that God left the temple, as has often been thought. When the Spirit descended from heaven in the baptismal vision, God did not leave heaven. If the early Christians had thought that God had withdrawn his presence from the temple in Jerusalem, they would not have continued to worship him there as they did (Acts 2:46; 3:1; 21:23–24). God did not leave the temple, but God is now equally present among his people, Jews and Gentiles, wherever they might be.

That should make it clear how appropriate it is that the declaration "Truly this man was God's Son" is made by a Gentile, the Roman centurion. (A centurion in the Roman army was not necessarily Roman by nationality, but he would certainly be a Gentile, not a Jew.) He was doubtless there at the cross because he was in charge of the group of soldiers who had crucified Jesus and stayed to see the job properly finished. It may be *appropriate* that this declaration should be made by a Gentile, but it is also very *surprising*. It is hard to tell what brought him to this conclusion. His words are ambiguous in the Greek: he could be saying, "This man was a son of God," or "This man was the Son of God." The former would be more plausible in the mouth of a pagan Gentile. The latter is what the Gospel has taught us as readers to think Jesus is, the absolutely unique Son of his divine Father. Perhaps Mark intends the ambiguity. The centurion meant as much as he could have understood within his non-monotheistic worldview. But we readers can see that he says more than he meant, the appropriate final revelation of Jesus's unique divine sonship in Mark's story.

(Mark says, "When the centurion . . . saw that in this way he breathed his last, he said, 'Truly this man was God's Son'" [15:39]. Some commentators take this to mean that the centurion was impressed by something about the way Jesus died. But probably Mark means only that it was after Jesus had breathed his last that the centurion gave, as it were, his verdict on the man. I doubt if we can know how he came to that verdict.)

Whatever his words might have meant to the centurion himself, what is clear is the significance of his declaration for our understanding of Mark's story of Jesus. We should recall that for Mark "Son of God" means much more than "the Messiah." Throughout the story many people have considered Jesus to be the Messiah, including the twelve disciples (8:29) and the crowds who hailed his entry into Jerusalem (11:9–10). But no human being has said that Jesus is the Son of God. This has previously been said only by God himself—in the baptismal vision and at the transfiguration—and by the demons who have supernatural knowledge about Jesus (3:11). No human being has perceived that Jesus is the Son of God until this point—at his death. Mark surely means us to see that we cannot really understand what it meant for Jesus to be the Son of God unless we accept—what his disciples found so difficult to accept—that being the Son entailed Jesus's suffering and death, the extreme pain, the extreme rejection, the extreme shame of this sort of death. Jesus was never more the divine Son of his heavenly Father than when he reached this extreme point of human degradation, reduced even to crying out that his Father had forsaken him (15:34).

Since we readers have heard God himself declare Jesus to be his beloved Son—at crucial points in the story and with revelatory power—we cannot doubt that Jesus remains God's beloved, dear to his Father's heart, even as the Father also leaves him to die in this abandoned way. For Jesus to bear the burden of humanity's sin and suffering, left by his Father to die, he had to be acting out of love for his Father, fulfilling his Father's will and making it his own will, and he had to be sustained by his Father's love for him at this supreme moment of their relationship. The three persons of the Trinity are not all explicitly present in the narrative of Jesus's death, but they are all implicit, as the story that began with the baptismal vision, the story of God's Trinitarian involvement with the world, reaches this climactic point.

Looking back over the three key moments of revelation in Mark's story, we can see that the first was a revelation to Jesus by his Father, the second a revelation by the Father to Jesus's disciples, but the third is really a revelation only to us, the readers. Whether the centurion is speaking to his fellow soldiers or just to himself scarcely matters. Mark gives us his words as a revelation to us. We are to see that Jesus is truly the Son of God in his death, in the extreme point of his following his Father's will for the salvation of the world. Having seen that, we can recapitulate the earlier revelations and read them as revelations not just to persons in the story but also to us. The mere fact that Mark has written them down for us makes that the case, of course.

What, in that case, do *we* make of the second moment of revelation, the one that climaxes with the words, "This is my beloved Son; listen to him!" (Mark 9:7)? How do we listen to Jesus? I said that for the disciples this meant listening to what Jesus had to say about his path to crucifixion and resurrection. The meaning is not that we should listen to Jesus's teaching in general, though I have no wish to downplay the importance of Jesus's teaching. The meaning is rather: Listen to Jesus's story as the Gospel tells it, the whole of his life and ministry and especially his path to the cross and his subsequent resurrection! Attend to that! The moments of revelation that frame the story are really telling us that the whole story is revelation to which we must attend.

Trinitarian Presence

By way of concluding this chapter, I should like to return to the theme of divine presence, to which the first chapter was devoted, thus bringing the argument of the book full circle. In the present chapter we have considered God as Trinity in his activity in the history of Jesus to accomplish salvation. We now turn to God as Trinity in the Christian experience of salvation, focusing on one of the most clearly Trinitarian texts in Paul's letters:

> The grace of the Lord Jesus Christ and the love of God
> and participation in the Holy Spirit be with you all.
> (2 Cor. 13:13 AT)

This benediction or "wish-prayer" (as it has been called) is an expansive example of the usually much shorter formula with which Paul concludes all his letters: "The grace of our Lord Jesus Christ be with you."[9] This formula occurs with a number of variations,[10] including the very abbreviated "Grace be with you."[11] But in all cases it is the grace of Jesus Christ that Paul wishes to be with his readers. Only in 2 Corinthians is the formula expanded to a Trinitarian form of blessing.

It is not sufficiently recognized that the blessing Paul desires for his readers in this formula is a form of divine presence. In the light of the abundant biblical usage that we examined in chapter 1, this must be the implication of the phrase "with you." The formula is modeled on the phrase, "The Lord (YHWH) be with you," which Paul actually uses in 2 Thessalonians 3:16 ("The Lord be with you all") and 2 Timothy 4:22 ("The Lord be with your spirit"). As frequently in Paul's writings, he takes "the Lord" (YHWH) of the Old Testament text to be Jesus. So the formula, "The grace of our Lord Jesus Christ be with you," effectively means: "May our Lord Jesus Christ in his grace be with you." He desires for his readers not simply "grace" as something detachable from its giver but the gracious presence of Jesus.

There is no obvious reason why Paul has expanded this formula into the threefold one that we find at the end of 2 Corinthians. Whatever the reason, he has given us a memorable expression of the threefold character of Christian experience of God. "Grace" and "love" are not necessarily assigned to Christ and God the Father respectively in Paul's usage: he can also associate grace with God and love with Christ. But they are perhaps most characteristically associated in the way they

9. This is the form used in 1 Thess. 5:28 and in 2 Thess. 3:18.

10. 1 Cor. 16:23; Gal. 6:18; Phil. 4:23; Philem. 25; cf. also Rev. 22:21.

11. Col. 4:18b; 1 Tim. 6:21b; 2 Tim. 4:22b; Titus 3:15b ("Grace be with all of you"); Eph. 6:24 ("Grace be with all who . . ."). It occurs also in Heb. 13:25 ("Grace be with all of you").

are here. "Grace" refers primarily to what Jesus Christ has done for us, his generous self-giving for us.[12] His gracious presence with us is as God become one of us, who lived, died, and was raised for us and who reaches out to us, his brothers and sisters. God the Father is the source of all love, who sent his Son and gave him up for us.[13] It is through Jesus that we come to know the Father's love. The Father's loving presence with us is as the divine love that fills our lives.[14]

The meaning of the third part of the benediction in 2 Corinthians is disputed. According to one interpretation, associated with the translation "the fellowship of the Holy Spirit," this third part refers to the fellowship among believers that is created by the Spirit. However, since it makes a better parallel with the other phrases by pointing like them to a relationship with God, it is more likely that the phrase means "participation in the Holy Spirit," referring to the participation in the presence and power of the Spirit that believers share. This is a different kind of divine presence in human life, though closely connected with the others. Paul's language in his various letters about the way we experience the three is quite fluid, but we do get the sense of a differentiated relationship in which God is present to us, with us, and in us in distinguishable ways.

12. E.g., Rom. 5:2; 2 Cor. 8:9; Gal. 1:6; 5:4.
13. E.g., Rom. 5:8; 8:32.
14. See Rom. 5:5.

Table 4.1
Three Key Moments of Revelation in Mark's Gospel

Prologue
Jesus's vision at his baptism (1:9–11)
Miracles
Peter's confession
First passion prediction
Transfiguration of Jesus (9:2–8)
Second and third passion predictions
Triumphal entry
Crucifixion
Temple veil and centurion's confession (15:37–39)
Burial and empty tomb

Table 4.2
Correspondences between the Three Key Moments of Revelation

Mark 1:9–11	Mark 9:2–8	Mark 15:34–39
baptism	transfiguration	cry of desolation
by John (= Elijah)	with Moses and Elijah	Elijah does not come
		Jesus dies (*exepneusen*)
heavens rent (*schizomenous*)	overshadowing cloud	temple veil rent (*eschisthē*)
Spirit (*pneuma*) descends on Jesus		
voice from heaven: "You are my beloved Son; with you I am well pleased."	voice from cloud: "This is my Son, listen to him!"	centurion: "Truly this man is the Son of God."

Bibliographic Notes

On the Trinity in Mark

Michael F. Bird, *Jesus the Eternal Son: Answering Adoptionist Christology* (Grand Rapids: Eerdmans, 2017), chap. 4.

Daniel Johansson, "The Trinity in the Gospel of Mark," in *The Essential Trinity: New Testament Foundations and Practical Relevance*, ed. Brandon D. Crowe and Carl R. Trueman (London: Inter-Varsity, 2016), 39–61.

On the Idea of the Trinitarian History of God with the World

Jürgen Moltmann, *The Trinity and the Kingdom of God: The Doctrine of God*, trans. Margaret Kohl (London: SCM, 1981), chap. 3.

On the Importance of the Prophecies of Isaiah in Mark

Joel Marcus, *The Way of the Lord: Christological Exegesis of the Old Testament in the Gospel of Mark* (Louisville: Westminster John Knox, 1992).

Rikki E. Watts, *Isaiah's New Exodus in Mark* (Grand Rapids: Baker, 1997).

Scripture and Ancient Writings Index

Old Testament

Genesis

Exodus

Job

Psalms

Isaiah

Jeremiah

Lamentations

Ezekiel

Daniel

Hosea